S. T. Hammond

Practical dog training, or, training vs. breaking

S. T. Hammond

Practical dog training, or, training vs. breaking

ISBN/EAN: 9783743313491

Manufactured in Europe, USA, Canada, Australia, Japa

Cover: Foto ©Lupo / pixelio.de

Manufactured and distributed by brebook publishing software (www.brebook.com)

S. T. Hammond

Practical dog training, or, training vs. breaking

FOREST AND STREAM SERIES, No. 2.

PRACTICAL
DOG TRAINING;

OR,

TRAINING VS. BREAKING.

BY

S. T. HAMMOND,

KENNEL EDITOR OF "FOREST AND STREAM."

NEW YORK:

FOREST AND STREAM PUBLISHING COMPANY,
39 PARK ROW.

1882.

Copyright, 1882, Forest and Stream Publishing Co.

NOTE.

The system of dog training described in this book is a new one. Its fundamental principles were adopted by the writer thirty years ago; the details of the method, as here given, have been developed and perfected by him during that time. His own success with it has encouraged the belief that its publication would be welcomed by the thousands of American sportsmen who own and handle field dogs. This belief, it is a pleasure to say, has been confirmed by the marked favor accorded to the successive chapters as they appeared in the FOREST AND STREAM, from which journal they are here reprinted.

This system is humane and rational. It is also practical and efficient. Dog training differs essentially from dog breaking, both in method and spirit, and also in what may be accepted as the test of all systems, namely: the results attained.

The pages of this book contain no theories. They are a plain, simple record of the plan which has been tested by the writer in the field, year after year. He believes that the same plan may be followed by others with equal success. It is, therefore, with the fullest confidence in the merits of this system of Dog Training *vs.* Dog Breaking, that it is submitted to the public.

The story of "My Old Dog Trim" is added, because from his day the author dates his conversion to the belief that training is better than breaking. The sketch of "The One-Eyed Grouse of Maple Run" is also given, that the reader may have in it some of the "reasons for the faith that is in us," when we advise the introduction of the youngsters to the haunts of this royal bird. These sketches are also given as illustrative of some of the pleasures enjoyed in the field in the companionship of a well-trained dog.   S. T. H.

FOREST AND STREAM OFFICE, March, 1882.

TRAINING VS. BREAKING.
Chapter I.

NEARLY all writers upon the subject of dog training appear to think that there is but one course to pursue. That all knowledge that is not beaten into a dog is worthless for all practical purposes, and that the whip, check-cord and spike-collar, with perhaps an occasional charge of shot or a vigorous dose of shoe leather, are absolutely necessary in order to perfect his education.

It may appear presumptuous for us to advocate a departure from the beaten path, but as we have had some little experience in the past thirty years, and as many sportsmen who should be good authority have seen our dogs at work, and have unanimously united in praise of the manner in which they acquit themselves in the field, we have thought that perhaps a description of our method of training might prove interesting. It will be so at least to the new beginner. The main object that we have in view is the amelioration of the present condition of "man's best friend," and should the perusal of these lines cause even but one to follow the course here marked out, we shall feel amply repaid for our labor.

We have ever been possessed of a great love deep down in the heart for our canine pets, and this love is the main spring that governs all our actions toward them. We do not wish to be understood as meaning that we never use the whip for we believe with the wise king of old that the rod should not be spared when it is needed. What we do mean is this: There is no dog worth the raising—we are speaking of pointers and setters—that cannot and will not learn all that it is necessary for him to know without a single blow being struck or a single harsh word being spoken. We are very well aware that this humane course will entail a little more labor, and that a vast deal more patience is required than when dependence is placed upon the whip and boot-heel to enforce your commands, but the intelligent and cheerful manner in which your pet obeys your slightest word or motion will much more than compensate you for the extra time that you have devoted to his education. There is nothing that so mars our enjoyment when in the field as to see the cringing form of a noble animal cowering in fear of a whipping, which nine times out of ten he does not deserve half so much as his master.

We do not claim absolute perfection for our system nor that you can by adopting it invariably succeed in turning out a well trained, well behaved dog, for we know that with dogs as well as with men we often find one who for lack of brains will never amount to much, no matter what pains we take with him.

In selecting a puppy there are many things to be taken into consideration. In the first place we must be sure that both sire and dam are first class field performers. This we consider of the utmost importance. They must also be possessed of endurance, and must be reasonably intelligent. The more ancestors of this type that our pup can boast the better will he suit us. He must also have life and ambition; indeed we care not how high strung he is, for although he may not submit to restraint quite so readily as his sleepy brother, yet when you once have him under subjection he will not only mind more quickly, but he will do his work better and much more of it. Of course he must be well formed, and we should like him to be of good color and coat, but these last are not indispensible as we much prefer good performance to good looks.

Having selected our pup, we will take him home when he is six to eight weeks old, and at once begin his education. Many writers will tell you that your dog should be much older before you begin to instil into his mind even the rudiments of knowledge. If you are going to pursue their system of instruction, we should advise you by all means to put off the evil day as long as possible; but if you are to follow our plan, begin at once; not a moment is to be lost. In the first place you want to secure his affection and entire confidence. This will be the first lesson, and nothing more should be attempted until you have completely won his heart and taught him to place the utmost confidence in you. At this tender age his mind is easily impressed, and will long retain the ideas now formed; and it will take but a few days to teach him to love you with all his heart. If possible, give him a good roomy pen on the ground, with a warm, well-sheltered house or box in which to lie. Do not forget that he will be very lonesome for a few days, and therefore glad to see you often; and you cannot better employ your time than in paying him a visit every half hour for the first day or two. Always, when you go to see him, have a bit of something for him to eat that he will relish. As you approach the pen you should invariably blow upon your whistle the note that you intend to use to call him in. We sound a long note for this purpose, beginning loud and gradually dying away. This, with a short, sharp note to attract attention, is all the signal that we ever sound upon the whistle; the last we do not use until his education is further advanced. By associating this long note with something good to eat, it will soon become fixed in his mind that when he hears it he must run to you as fast as he can. We much prefer to have two pups, for it takes no more time to teach them both than it does to teach one, as they will learn from each other; and if one is inclined to be dilatory we withold his reward, and he, seeing the other one enjoying his customary allowance while he is himself deprived of his share, at once comprehends the true reason and will be on hand the next time.

Do not fail to abundantly caress him and speak kindly words, and never under any circumstances, no matter what the provocation, allow yourself to scold or strike him, as this is entirely at variance with our system, and is sure to result in the defeat of our plans. Should he jump upon you with his dirty feet, or tear your clothes with his sharp teeth, do not get angry and cuff him, but gently yet firmly place him upon the ground or unclasp his jaws from your garments, consoling yourself with the thought that in a short time you will have him so well in hand that he will know better than to commit these faults. Be very gentle with him at all times; carefully study his disposition, and learn all of his ways that you may the more readily understand just how to manage him. You should be in perfect sympathy with him and humor all his whims and notions and endeavor to teach him that you truly love him. In a short time you will find that this love will be returned ten fold, and that he is ever anxiously watching for your coming, and never so happy as when in your presence and enjoying your caresses.

After a few days you may begin to train him, but do not be in a hurry about it, as nothing is gained by haste. Be very careful now, and do not ruin all by an undue haste; go very slow, carefully feel your way, and, above all things, exercise an unwearied patience; and if at any time you find the strain upon your nerves growing a little too tense, leave him at once and wait until you are perfectly calm before resuming the lesson.

There is one thing, of the utmost importance, that we wish to particularly impress upon your mind before we go any further. Do not allow yourself under any circumstances to speak to your pupil in anything but your ordinary tone of voice. There is nothing that is more annoying when shooting than to have a companion continually yelling at the top of his voice to his dog, and generally without any effect. Now, such yelling is worse than useless, for if your dog is properly trained in the first place, he will readily mind your lightest word. For your own comfort, then, and for the pleasure of whoever may accompany you upon your shooting excursions, use nothing but gentle tones when you issue your commands. When this very disagreeable habit of shouting is once commenced, you will soon find that a still louder tone is demanded, and had you the lungs of a Stentor, it will not be long before your resources will be exhausted, and you will vainly sigh for thunder tones to voice your words of command.

The first thing that we endeavor to teach a pup, after we obtain his love and confidence, is to stop at the words *To ho*. This is a very important point, and comparatively easy to teach him. He should be very hungry when you commence these first lessons, as his eagerness for the food will cause him to pay you close attention; and when he understands that as soon as he performs his task his reward is sure, and that he cannot have it before, he will anxiously strive to do whatever you may require of him. You should begin by giving him a taste of a piece of meat, then secure a firm hold upon his collar, and place a small piece upon the ground in front of him. He will struggle with all his strength to get at it, but hold him steadily, and do not say a word until he becomes partially quiet; then move his nose a little nearer, and, in your ordinary tone of voice, say *To ho*, with a falling accent upon the last syllable. Do not repeat the words just yet, and when you do be very careful that your voice is not strained and unnatural; we always accompany this word with the right hand raised warningly, for it may often happen that we wish our dog to come to a halt at some distance from us, and by accustoming him to the gesture he will soon learn to stop as far as he can see you. Most sportsmen use this signal to make their dogs charge, but as we shall show further on, when we come to it, the other plan is much better. After a few seconds the dog will become more quiet, and you can repeat the words. Now carefuly watch him, and as soon as his attention is fixed upon the meat, and he looks at it steadily for a second, release your hold and cluck to him as a signal that he can now have it, and at once praise and pet him, and give him to understand that he has done something wonderful, and that you are pleased with him. We should have stated before that, from the first, whenever you place his food before him you should always cluck to him, as he will thus learn the meaning of the sound, and understand when he hears it that all restraint is removed.

After the first trial do not try him again until the next time that you feed him; for should you force him he may grow weary and fail to respond with that cheerfulness and alacrity that is so pleasing to see. You must be very careful that he does not get at the meat until you give him permission, for he must understand that you mean business every time, and that he cannot have it until he becomes perfectly quiet and hears your signal. After a few lessons of this kind, if you have managed right, you will be surprised to see the improvement that he will make and the zest with which he will enter into the spirit of it. You can soon leave him free, and he will readily point at the word; and with proper care he will soon learn to point when the meat is thrown to quite a distance from him. Of course you will understand that the distance must be increased very gradually, and implicit obedience exacted every time. Should he move so much as one step after you give him the word, you must instantly place him as near as may be in his former position, at the same time repeating the word; and this must be done gently yet firmly until he becomes steadfast. Too much importance cannot be attached to this; indeed, it is the groundwork of our whole system; and unless you thoroughly instill into his mind the knowledge that you mean just what you say, and must be obeyed to the very letter, and that he cannot vary the fraction of an inch from the rule that you have laid down, it will not be of any use to continue further, for under our system—or any other—it will be utterly impossible to turn out a well trained animal unless we strictly adhere to the above rule and exact implicit obedience every time.

After he once undertstands that he must mind, your task is half accomplished, the rest is comparatively easy, and you will indeed find it a labor of love to perfect his education.

In giving these first lessons do not remove him from his pen, as new surroundings will serve to distract his attention from the business on hand, and your task will be all the harder. Indeed it is much better to avoid all training outside the pen until your pupil is well established in what you have taught him. Should it not be convenient to have a pen for him, any good sized room or inclosure that he cannot get out of, will answer for training purposes. Do not allow any spectators in these first lessons, as you want his undivided attention. We know that there is great satisfaction in showing off the little fellow's accomplishments to one's friends, but until you are quite sure that he will obey when strangers are near, it is much better to practice him alone than to have him go back on you before folks where you might feel a little delicacy about enforcing your commands.

CHAPTER II.

CANINE ACCOMPLISHMENTS.

WHILE teaching our pup to charge, his other lesson must by no means be neglected, but plenty of practice must be sandwiched in until he appears to thoroughly understand the meaning of *To ho*, and will readily stop at the word or upraised hand. When he is reasonably perfect in this, you can vary the lesson by placing the food upon your knee, as you sit by him, and bringing his nose very close to it, and after a while, as he improves, you can lay the morsel upon his nose and he will soon learn to hold perfectly still and retain any attitude that you may place him in. As he advances in knowledge, you should take a piece of meat of good size, that he cannot swallow, and carefully open his mouth—this you can do by clasping your hand around his muzzle and gently forcing the thumb and fingers between his jaws—and placing the piece therein, at the same time commanding him to *To ho*. Do not remove your hand from his jaws, but hold him lightly yet firmly; for although the chances are in favor of his understanding what is wanted, and obeying readily, still it is necessary to retain the grasp as we are not through with him yet; and should the taste of the meat prove too tempting and he undertake to bolt it, you, having a good hold of him, can at once open his mouth and secure the meat. As soon as he comprehends what you require and remains perfectly quiet, gently force open his mouth and take the meat from him, at the same time telling him to "drop," and at once reward him with a piece of some other kind of meat, thus teaching him that he cannot eat the first piece, nor even mouth it, but must deliver it safe into your hand. We generally use a piece of tough, partly-cooked beef for the trial, and are very particular in our first lessons of this kind to reward him with a bit of liver or something entirely different from the large piece. The utility of this lesson we will explain further on, only remarking here that we consider it of vital importance that our pupil should be thoroughly trained in this, for we think it to be one of his most necessary lessons, and too much time cannot be expended in perfecting him in this branch of his education. He should become so perfect in this that he will take the smallest bit of meat in his mouth and hold it perfectly still, without the slightest movement of his jaws, and deliver it readily into your hand without reluctance.

You should accustom him to the restraint of the chain very early in his career, for the longer you wait the harder will be the task; he should be chained up two or three times each day, for a little while only at a time, taking care that he is perfectly quiet when you loose him. Should he be very restless and uneasy, you must soothe him with kind words and pet him until he becomes quiet, and on no account unfasten him until he ceases his struggles and remains calm for a little while, thus teaching him that howlings and strugglings will not set him free. Be very careful to see that he cannot break his collar nor slip it over his head, nor break his chain, for it is of the utmost importance that your lessons should be thorough, and that at no time should he get the idea into his head that there is any possible course except implicit obedience to your wishes. Great care must be taken at all times, in all his lessons, that he is not kept under restraint for too long a time, but the increase of time must be none the less sure, although very gradual and almost imperceptible. Much will depend upon his disposition in this, which, if you have carefully studied, you will be able to manage, so that he shall not become disgusted and be an unwilling pupil. At the slightest indication that he is getting weary of instruction, you must let up a little and proceed slower, but with such care and good judgment that he shall not mistrust the reason; and if you pursue the proper course and manage him rightly, you will be amply repaid when he comes to maturity in witnessing the intelligent and cheerful manner in which he will obey your commands and submit to long-continued restraint without a murmur.

We accustom our pup from the first to the society of

fowls, and if possible procure a brood of chickens for him to associate with. We greatly prefer game fowls for this purpose, for we think they are possessed of stronger scent, thus being more attractive to him, and making him all the more eager to investigate them, while the mother being much more brave in their defense than a common dunghill will at his first attempt to chase or worry them give him a lesson that he will never forget. Upon the occasion of his first introduction to them, do not allow him to mistrust that you have planned the interview, but let him accidentally come upon them while at play ; he may not chase, but the chances are that he will make a rush for them. Do not stir, but calmly say, *To ho*, and leave the rest to the old hen. Should he hear you and stop, you must caress and praise him. Should he "point" them, do not encourage, neither must you prevent him, but take no notice of it, for should he find that it was pleasing to you he might form habits that would not always prove satisfactory. On the other hand, should you discourage him he would perhaps think it was wrong to point, so that the best way is to leave him alone, and let him point to his heart's content, thankful that he has the instinct, and content to patiently await the proper time to so direct this wonderful gift that its display shall minister to your pleasure and afford you abundant enjoyment.

There is one other point to which we wish to call your attention while we are upon the subject. If you have hunted much you have undoubtedly seen dogs that would point rabbits and perhaps chase them. Now, that our pupil may not be guilty of such indiscretion, when old enough to take the field, we will proceed to so train him that he will never pay them the slightest attention. We always obtain, if possible, a pair or more of our common wild rabbits; if these cannot be had the tame variety will answer. Then we build them a hutch alongside the puppy's pen, with a hole communicating just large enough for them to pass through, that they may visit him at their pleasure and readily escape should he be too familiar, and our word for it you never need fear that your dog is pointing a rabbit. We once purchased for a song a magnificent dog, which was entirely worthless from this cause. Although he had an excellent nose, and was perfectly staunch, he would point every rabbit that came in his way, and would "draw" on their trail, and you could never make sure but he was leading you after one of these pests instead of a bird. We took him home and placed him in a large yard, with several of his bob-tailed friends, and left him to his fate. He pointed them steadily all the afternoon, and refused to leave them to eat his supper. What he did during the night we cannot say, but when we visited him in the morning, although he was lying down, he was still staunchly pointing, but apparently very tired. He did leave them long enough to eat his breakfast, but as soon as it was down he immediately resumed his work. This went on for nearly a week before he appeared to weaken, and before the close of the second week he evidently had had enough of it. We then took him into the field, taking pains to go where rabbits were plenty, but not once did he pay them the slightest attention, nor was he ever known to notice them again. For the same reason we like to have cats about the house that our pup may become well acquainted with them before he commences hunting.

We should have mentioned before that the pup should be let out of his pen for a good run, at least twice a day, and if he will remain about the house and not stray away, we should much prefer to let him run all the time, for the more exercise that he gets the better will it be for his strength and endurance in the future, and the less he is confined the better will it be for his courage and confidence.

While our pup is yet young he should be taught to love the sound of the gun. This can be easily accomplished if the proper course is pursued. In the first place we take a couple of old tin pans, and while his attention is attracted by something that interests him we strike them together, lightly at first; and if he appears to be afraid we are very careful not to add to his fright by a repetition of the noise anywhere near him, but take the pans to quite a distance from his pen and leave them, and wait awhile before trying again. When it is time to feed him we go to the pans, and while sounding our whistle, as before described, to let him know that we are coming, we give a stroke just loud enough for him to hear plainly, and at once proceed to his pen and give him his feed. By pursuing this course for a few days, and gradually going a little closer every time, he will become accustomed to the sound, and learning that the noise is connected with our coming, and also his dinner, he soon gets used to it, and in a short time will stand the racket without flinching. When he has become so accustomed to the noise that he shows no signs of fear at quite a loud crash it is time to try him with the gun. In order to do this understandingly you will require an assistant. Let him take the gun loaded with a light charge of powder and stand at some little distance—say forty or fifty yards away—and be ready at your signal to fire. You will now enter his pen, and after he gets a little quiet call him to you and put a piece of meat before him and bid him *Toho*, at the same time raising your hand as a signal for the gun. Carefully watch him, and should he display any sign of fear the experiment must be repeated as with the pans. There is no need of your presence only to notice how he behaves, and you can dispense with your assistant, unless, as will probably be the case, he does not mind the report, when the gun can be brought nearer, and you can make another trial. Great care must be taken not to frighten him with too loud a discharge, nor should it be too close to him, until he gets used to it. By paying close attention to him when under fire, you can readily tell how far it will do to go, and by properly conducting your experiment you can soon teach him to love the sound of the gun, even when fired over his head; indeed we have cured in this way some of the worst cases of gun-shyness that we ever saw. Comparatively few dogs are gun-shy, and it is with these only that those precautions are necessary. After your pup has been carefully accustomed to the noise do not lay the gun aside as soon as you have accomplished your object, but let him hear the sound occasionally until his education is complete, taking good care that the discharge of the gun is at once followed by something pleasing to him—his dinner, for instance—or let it be a prelude to giving him his liberty, thus giving him to understand that the noise means something, and soon the noise, or even the sight of the gun, will cause him pleasurable emotions that he will never forget.

CHAPTER III.

CHARGE!

WE will take it for granted that, after a week or two of daily practice, our pupil has so far advanced in his education as to be reasonably proficient in his performance at *To ho*, and we will now take another step and try him with something new, and endeavor to teach him the meaning of the word *charge*. As this word is in constant use among sportsmen the world over, we always teach our dogs its meaning; but for our own use we greatly prefer a low breathed *Sh!* It is just as effective and far more quiet, especially when you take your dog into company, for instead of attracting the attention of every one in the room by commanding him to charge, you can give him this signal, and scarcely one even of those nearest you will notice it. We have used this for more than twenty years, and can heartily recommend it. Most persons train their dogs to charge at the upraised hand. We do not quite like this, and have never adopted the custom, for it very seldom occurs that you wish your dog to drop at any great distance from you, but should you from any cause wish your dog to remain quiet when he is at a distance, how much better it is to teach him to come to a full stop at the raising of your hand, and remain upon his feet when he can see you and be ready to obey your next signal. Even at the discharge of the gun or rise of the bird, we greatly prefer that the dog, instead of charging, should instantly stop and stand up, where he can readily see what is going on. There are many arguments in favor of this course that we will not mention until we get further on.

We will now take our pupil in hand and see if we can teach him to "charge." Place one hand upon his shoulders and neck and the other upon his hips, and gently, yet firmly, force him to a recumbent position, at the same time repeat the word *charge*, prefaced with the low *sh—*. Do not forget to use only your natural tone, at the same time the word must be spoken in a decided way that cannot be mistaken for entreaty instead of command. This word must not be spoken more than once, and given with a falling inflection; keep him in position until he ceases struggling and his muscles relax. After a second or two, if he remains quiet, remove your hands and allow him to get up. By using the words "hold up" or "get up" in this connection he will soon learn their meaning; but do not do this until he appears to understand what you want of him, and on no account, no matter how long the struggle continues, should you repeat the word, nor let up on him one particle, for everything depends on first impressions, and as soon as your pupil finds that his struggles to escape avail him nothing, and that relentless as fate you are bound to conquer and accomplish your purpose, he will at each successive lesson be more willing to yield. To this persistent painstaking and unwearied perseverance in sticking to our point until our object is accomplished do we owe much of our success in training.

We must again repeat that all this time you must keep perfectly cool, and must suffer no sign to escape you of anger or impatience; for if you cannot control your temper you are not the one to train a dog, and had better resort to the breaking process at once.

Great care should be taken to place the pup in a natural position. When you force him down see that his hind legs are squarely under his body and his fore-legs advanced well in front, with the head resting between or upon them, and always insist upon this position.

In the first few lessons it is not necessary to keep him in position more than a second or two, but be very careful that he understands that you are to be the judge of the proper time when he may get up. As he grows older the time can be very gradually extended, according to his disposition. Should he be very nervous and excitable, great care must be had that he does not get heart-broken with unnecessary and long continued restraint.

Do not expect that he will at once become perfect in any.

thing that you may teach him, but possess your soul in patience and allow and encourage him to act out his puppy ways and to play and frolic to his heart's content, always excepting, of course, the few moments that you devote to his lessons. Above all things, carefully refrain from anything that looks like restraint in your ordinary intercourse with him, and endeavor to instill into his mind that you are his loving friend, and that nothing suits you better than to see him thoroughly enjoy himself. We have found by experience that dogs are very much like men in some respects. They both are possessed of a superabundance of steam that must have vent somehow, and it is much better to get rid of the surplus while your pupil is of too tender an age to work any serious harm, than to bottle it up for escape in the future, when added years and knowledge are very prone to turn the current into dangerous channels. How much better it is to allow your boy to chase the gaudy butterfly and to encourage him to renewed efforts and let him learn for himself, that even if he is successful in securing the object of his desire, that the chase is futile and will not pay for bruised and tired limbs and soiled and torn clothes—how much better this than to keep him unwilling at your side, with his young heart almost bursting to essay the trial and sowing the seed that in a few years will ripen and cause him at the first opportune moment to break, not for butterflies now, but in a wild chase for forbidden pleasures that the restraints of his childhood make doubly dear. Do not think that we are moralizing; we are only illustrating. Therefore, when your pupil gives chase to the "butterflies of youth," do not check him, but rather urge him on, that he may the sooner discover the fallacy of the pursuit. In the meantime console yourself with the thought that he is working off his surplus steam and will all the sooner settle down to the real duties of life and do you no discredit by wild escapades in his mature years.

There is one thing that we consider of paramount importance—our pup must staunchly point when he is from six to ten weeks old. If he will not do this naturally and of his own free will, quickly dispose of him to some one who is not so particular, and try again. Although his breeding may be of the best and the chances in favor of his pointing in the future, still there are so many elements of chance in raising up dogs that we should strive to eliminate at least all of the doubtful ones. We have yet to see the dog that would make a gamy point at this tender age who would not fulfill the promise in his riper years; while "the woods are full of them" that, having passed their youth without displaying this "heaven born gift" still make no sign. It is not necessary that he should be tried on game birds—although this is desirable—but any bird will answer the purpose; a fowl or chicken will do first-rate, or almost anything that will attract his attention so that he makes a staunch point. Do not force this upon him, but merely give him a chance to discover the bird or chicken himself, and if he has this instinct implanted within him you may depend upon his showing it. Many pups who will staunchly point at this age may, perhaps, a few weeks or months later, show no sign; give yourself no uneasiness on this account, for you know that the instinct is there and, although it may be dormant for a while, you can rest secure that it will return in proper season.

Do not forget during all your lessons, and while at play with him, to pet and fondle him; but do not allow him to jump upon you at any time. Whenever he does this you should at once firmly remove him and he will soon learn that this will not do. You should also talk to him—not baby talk—but use intelligent, rational language, just such as you would use in talking to a ten year old boy, and you will be surprised to see how soon he will understand your conversation. We are well aware that many persons will ridicule this, and will claim that a dog should be taught just as little as will answer to make him understand his duties while in the field, and that what they term "fancy training" is a positive injury to his usefulness. We have no sympathy with these views, for nearly all of the pleasure derived from our shooting trips is in witnessing the intelligent manner in which our pets perform their duties, and well satisfied are we that the more varied their accomplishments and the more developed their reasoning faculties, the more enjoyment will they afford. That many writers of renown disagree with us upon this point is true; and formerly, while perusing the finished productions of their able pens, we have been haunted by lingering doubts that after all perhaps they were right and that our system was open to serious objections; but after a tramp over the stubble or through the covert with these same writers, and witnessing the delight with which they gazed upon the performance of our dogs, and listening to the lavish encomiums which they bestowed upon their good behavior, we have been confirmed in the faith that our system is not radically wrong, to say the least. Many sportsmen whom we have met in the field insist upon congratulating us upon the wonderful good luck that we have had in obtaining such intelligent animals. That they are intelligent is plain to be seen; that they are naturally more so than thousands of others we cannot believe, for we have had considerable experience with many strains of both pointers and setters. Of pointers we have owned the "gazelle-eyed," satin-coated, light weight beauties, and many of the different strains and crosses up to the lumbering Spaniard; and of setters we have cultivated the "wild Irishman," as well as his more staid English and Scotch brothers, together with many animals of our grand old native stock, and have ever found them all endowed with faculties that needed but proper training to develop them into intelligent companions as well as first class "killing" dogs.

We will now return to our pupil, whom we have given quite a rest—and continue our lessons, ever remembering that we must "hasten slowly," and not over-burden his youthful days with care and sorrow by too frequent or long continued restraint. Unless he is very dull and stupid, or inclined to be refractory, or worse than all, sulky, a very short time is sufficient to give him all the instruction and practice needed, indeed the shorter the time occupied in his lessons at this tender age the better, provided you succeed in obtaining an intelligent obedience to your commands.

You should be pretty well acquainted with his disposition by this time, and be able to form an opinion as to whether it will pay to keep him or try again. We are very loth to expend much time with a dull or stupid one, and a sour or sulky disposition we abominate, and dispose of such as soon as may be. We are best suited when a pup is full of life and shows that he has a will of his own. We care not if he be headstrong, even willful, so that he is full of life and action, for we have ever found that these high-strung animals are not only possessed of greater intelligence than their less sensitive companions, but as a rule they are more killing dogs, to say nothing of the greater pleasure that they afford by their superior style of going. Should his temperament appear to be what you desire, thankfully proceed with your pleasurable task.

You must be careful when you commence his lesson that you do not cross him by beginning when he has something of importance upon his mind that will distract his attention from the business on hand; if he is busy with a bone, or engaged at play or his mind appears to be preoccupied, leave him quietly alone until he is disengaged, and then go on with the lesson; by pursuing this course you will secure his undivided attention, and not only save time. but much wear and tear of your stock of patience, it will be time enough to teach him that he must leave his bone or cease his play at your command when he is a little older and a little further advanced in his education; at the same time should you unthinkingly order him to do anything while he is engaged, you must see to it that the order is obeyed at all hazards, for it will never do to play fast-and-loose with him, nor to allow him to get the idea into his head that he can ever have his own way, when you desire the contrary. After you have taught him to charge readily without the aid of your hand to force him down, you can gradually increase your distance from him when you give the order; and if you are very careful to make him instantly obey you, and do not allow him to take even a single step after the command is given, he will soon obey the order as far as he can hear your voice.

CHAPTER IV.

THE WHISTLE AGAIN!

WHEN our pupil has become so well established in the knowledge of what is required of him that he will, when at quite a distance from you, instantly stop at the signal of the upraised hand and retain his position until given permission to move, we will advance him another step, and teach him the meaning of that other sound of the whistle, that we have mentioned as being used to attract his attention. We always use for this purpose two very short, quick toots, with the second one following the first instantly. As the meaning of this signal is entirely different from the one that he has become accustomed to, so should the sound be also so different that he can never mistake the one from the other, nor for an instant be in doubt as to what is required of him when he hears the sound of the whistle.

As much depends upon first impressions, we will take good care that we start right, and that we let him hear the first sound of this signal at an opportune moment, and as we wish to teach him that this sound is only to attract his attention, we will be very careful that he is not looking toward us, but wait until he is at some little distance from us, and looking the other way. At the same time care must be taken that he is not particularly engaged about anything that would tend to distract his mind. At just the right time you should sound the signal in a short, sharp, quick way, but only loud enough for him to hear distinctly, and he will at once look around to learn what this means. At the instant he casts his eye in your direction, raise your hand as a signal for him to *To ho*. Be very sure that your hand is raised at the proper time, for, as we have remarked before, first impresssions are very important, particularly in this lesson, and he should instantly see and obey your signal, thus learning— if this course is always pursued—that the two short blasts mean nothing in themselves, and are only a warning to call his attention to something of importance that you wish him to do.

You will find it necessary to vary this or he will come to associate this signal with your command of *To ho*, and at once stop when he hears it. Now we wish to train him so thoroughly in this that, when we come, a little later, to teach him to quarter his ground, he will not slacken his speed at the sound, but merely turn his head in your direction, and quick as a flash obey whatever signal you may give him; therefore, when you repeat this lesson, instead of raising your hand for him to stop, command him to charge. Of course you will see that he is near enough to hear you plainly. Perhaps it will be as well at the next trial to sound the long note as soon as he looks around, and call him in, not forgetting to abundantly caress and praise him when he performs his task in a pleasing manner. We think it a very good plan to always have in our pocket something good for him to eat, and when he minds this long note and comes in quickly, we reward him with a bit of something substantial as well as with fine words. This system of rewards must not be carried too far nor practiced too often, but used occasionally when he performs his duties in a satisfactory manner; especially when he comes in at the sound of the whistle quickly and cheerfully, a little piece of meat will at least have no tendency to slacken his speed when next he hears this signal. This instantaneous, almost electric obedience and cheerful alacrity is most pleasing to witness, especially when hunting in company with others whose dogs may not be quite up to the standard in this respect. Therefore no pains should be spared to so perfect our pupil in this, so that when we come to practical work in the field his actions shall cause us no disquiet nor reflect discredit upon our skill as his teacher.

There is one word more that our pupil should early become accustomed to, and it will be well to introduce its use almost at the beginning. This is the word *On*. You can use this word alone or, as many prefer, you can say *Go on* or *Hie on*. Either or all are well enough, and your pup will learn the meaning just as quickly even should you indiscriminately use all three, as it is the word *on* every time, and even if you should paraphrase it, as a well known sportsman is in the habit of doing, and order you dog to *Git on*, it will make no difference.

Let us charge you once more to be sure and issue all your commands in a decided manner, and always in your ordinary tone of voice; and do not fail to deliver each one with a falling inflection, for we never yet saw the man who issued his orders with a rising inflection but was sadly bothered to have them obeyed. By using this word, or any of the above variations, when you cluck to him to take his food, he will soon understand its meaning if the word instantly follows the cluck. Probably he will get the two mixed at first, but as you practice him at *To ho*, he will soon learn what it means; for as he improves in this and becomes steady, he should be taught to point at gradually increased distances, and the word *On* should be used to move him up; and in a short time, if this is properly managed, he will carefully and steadily "draw" on a piece of meat for a long distance. Great care must be had that you do not confuse him by seemingly contradictory orders, for he now thinks that your cluck and *On* mean one and the same thing, and in order to teach him the difference you must omit the cluck when you wish him to advance, and omit the *On* when you wish him to eat the morsel before him. This can be readily accomplished by placing the meat four or five feet from him, and after he has pointed it a short time tell him to *Go on*, and when he is close to it make him *To ho* once more; and then cluck to him as a signal that he may have it. We always partially omit the *On* after the cluck, as soon as he appears to understand its meaning, only using it enough to keep him from forgetting it, and as soon as we begin to teach him the difference we are very careful not to use either one in place of the other, until he has the lesson well learned and appears to thoroughly understand both signals, when we can safely mix them again; for oftentimes when shooting we may wish to move him on, especially when trailing ruffed grouse when the capture of the bird depends upon our absolute silence, at least so far as words are concerned; therefore he should be taught to advance at the sound of the cluck as well as the word *On*.

When well accustomed to the restraint of the chain, he should be taught to come to heel and quietly walk by your side. We greatly prefer that our dog should keep this position with his head just opposite our legs, where we can see him without turning around, instead of having him behind us. In order to teach him this, quickly and well, you should procure a stick, about two feet long and an inch in diameter, and fasten a snap at one end of it. This you can easily accomplish with the aid of a bit of leather. Now spring the snap into the ring in his collar and take a little walk with him. We generally manage a few of these first lessons at his usual meal time by placing his dish of food at the proper distance before we take him in hand. He should know nothing of his dinner until you lead him to it. When all is ready take a firm hold of your end of the stick and walk along at your usual gait, coaxing him to follow. Be sure and have the stick at the right angle to keep him just where you intend to have him go. After one or two steps, and when you have got him well under way, you must say *Heel* to him, and repeat the word once or twice as you walk along. You cannot expect that his behavior will be entirely faultless upon the first trial, but no matter how he takes it, lead him straight to his dinner and at once unfasten him and let him eat. After a few lessons of this kind, he will become perfectly reconciled, and you can gradually extend your walk and occasionally omit giving his food at the end, and he will soon learn to keep his place without the aid of the stick. Then you can extend your walks, taking care to be very gradual in the increase of time, and to be very sure that he implicitly obeys you and does not leave his place for even so much as a second's time, until you bid him go on. If this lesson is thoroughly—now do not smile at my frequent repetition of this word, for it is a word that we are very fond of, and one that we wish to *thoroughly* impress upon your mind as being of the greatest importance in perfecting our pupil in his education—if this lesson is thoroughly learned, you will be spared much trouble and worry in the future. Should you have occasion to walk the streets, you will not be obliged to whistle at every turn, and perhaps to wait and search for your dog, but you will know just where he is and what he is doing. Then how much better is it, when you come to the practical application of the knowledge, which you have been to so much trouble to impart, and take your dog into the field, to have him quietly retain his position by your side instead of rushing wildly around at his own sweet will, and compelling you to shout yourself hoarse and to unstring your nerves in a continual struggle to keep him within bounds, thus placing you at a double disadvantage, for the continual noise not only frightens the birds, causing them to rise out of shot, but the constant worry of mind and strain upon the nerves is a very prolific source of unsteadiness in shooting.

Do not neglect giving your pupil plenty of practice at all his lessons, as well as the one just commenced; not wearying nor long continued practice, but just enough to keep him well up to his work. If you have a spare moment give him a little turn at *To ho*, ever aiming at perfection; and be sure to see that he does his work well, and never allow him to perform his task in a careless or slovenly manner. You should also practice him at *Charge*, until he will not only obey the order readily, but retain his position in a perfectly quiet manner until you shall bid him *Hold up*.

He should be made to *Charge* when you are out walking with him; and taught to remain quiet, while you walk around; and in a short time you can go quite a distance, even out of his sight, and he will patiently await your return. Your orders should be given at unexpected times, when he is not looking for them. By this course you will teach him to be always ready to obey, no matter when nor where he may hear the signal. He should also be taught to hold his position at *To ho*, while you walk around and away from him; for it frequently happens, when trailing birds, that you wish to go round to avoid a mud hole or brier patch, and if your dog has been well trained in this, by witnessing one intelligent performance of this p'easing accomplishment, you will be more than repaid for all labor expended in teaching it to him.

Many dogs will pay no attention to strangers, and appear to care for no one except their masters. Should your pup be inclined to notice others, and give you any trouble in this respect, you can very easily teach him better, by having some one call the dog to him, and give him a few light cuts with a switch; and by changing your assistant every time, and administering two or three doses of this, he will give you no further trouble. If your assistants will fondle him a little before administering the switch, the pup will all the sooner find out that it is better to have nothing to do with others than yourself, and will not bother you later by running to every one who may notice him.

CHAPTER V.

QUARTERING.

WHAT is more pleasing to the eye of the sportsman than the evolutions of a well-trained dog as he systematically quarters his ground? With what satisfaction and pleasure we gaze upon his graceful motions as with head high in air he gallops across the wind, ever turning at the signal or the promptings of his own good judgment, and crossing just in front covers the whole ground! Pardonable, indeed, is the pride of the sportsman who possesses such an animal, for well we know how rare it is to see this performance in perfection.

Many dogs seem to possess a sort of instinct for this, and without any special training will quarter their ground very fairly; while others appear to have no inherent sense of the matter, but will beat straight ahead in whatever direction they are started, and neither turn to the right nor left, nor stop until they find scent, or are recalled by the whistle. Should your pup prove to be of the former class, thank your lucky stars for the kindly fortune; but relax not your efforts to so train him that his performance shall be faultless. On the other hand, should he display no aptitude for this, do not despair, for with proper training he can be taught to acquit himself very fairly, so well, in fact, that his performances will compare favorably with those of a large majority of other dogs that he may meet in the field.

Before commencing his lessons in quartering our pupil should fully understand the meaning of the word "*On*," and readily move forward on hearing it. He will also have acquired some knowledge of the meaning of the motion of your hand as indicating the direction that you wish him to take from the practice that you have given him at "*To ho.*" For when you have thrown the piece of meat for him to point, he has noticed that this motion is invariably in the direction that he saw the meat thrown, and as he is possessed of reasoning faculties of no mean order, he has figured it all out and has arrived at correct conclusions in the matter, and you will find upon trial that he will readily start in the direction you wish him to take at the first wave of your hand.

While instructing him in this branch of his education we may as well improve the opportunity to get his head in the air where it belongs, for when we get in the field with him we shall find this accomplishment to be very desirable; indeed, I always adopt this plan from the first in his practice at " *To ho*" unless he is naturally high-headed; and even then it can do no harm. You must be sure that he is well advanced in the lessons already taught before you attempt to teach him this. Then when he is very hungry take him into a large yard, or still better into some open field where you will be free from interruption by any one, and having provided yourself with two kinds of meat (as mentioned in his first lesson at " *To ho*") and also with two or three sticks about two feet long and as thick as your finger and sharpened at each end, you are ready to commence operations. You should always enter the field from the leeward side as in actual hunting; and after making your pupil charge, you will walk away from him about twenty yards. Do not go directly up wind but diagonally across; thus, if the wind is west you will go to the northwest or southwest, as you may prefer; and after impaling a piece of meat upon the end of one of the sticks, set the other end in the ground just firm enough to remain in position. I think that it is better to set it in a bunch of grass or low bushes, that it may be hid from his sight, as it is time to teach him that he must depend upon his nose. If there are no bushes handy you can easily carry with you a few leafy twigs, or if in winter a few pine boughs, and stick down one or two in front to hide it from view. In this way place one or two more pieces at some little distance from the first one and also from each other, taking care to put them so that you can work up wind toward them, and be sure that you do not forget their location.

Now return to your pupil and praise and pet him for his

good behavior in remaining quiet, and reward him with a bit of the same kind of meat that is on the stick. After he has eaten it, and is intently watching for more, take another piece of the same kind and let him smell of it; and then make believe throw it in the direction that you wish him to go, which should be at an angle from the meat upon the stick; thus, if the stick is northwest from you, make the motion toward the north, which will take him across the wind and also bring him near enough to the meat to smell it when he gets opposite it. Carefully watch him and the very instant that he strikes the scent you must make him *To ho;* then walk up to him and praise and pat him, but make him hold his position while you advance and pick up the stick and take the meat therefrom and put it in your pocket, taking good care that he has a good view of the whole performance. Now abundantly reward him with praise and give him a piece of the other kind of meat to eat.

After a few moments' rest you can proceed to look for the next piece in the same manner, and if he shows no sign of weariness you can continue to the third. Beyond this I do not think it advisable to go at the first lesson, nor even so far if he shows the least sign of having had enough of it. Indeed, in all his lessons and practice it is much better to stop far short of satiety than to weary and perhaps disgust him with too long continued application. Your own good judgment will generally tell you when to stop, and you will find that five minutes', or even one minute's practice, that leaves your pupil in a happy frame of mind induced by the bestowal of your well merited praise is much better than an hour's that finds you both fagged out and disheartened by the failure to accomplish satisfactory results. We have learned by experience that the shorter the time devoted to his lessons the better, provided that he is practiced every day, several times if you like, and a satisfactory performance of his task obtained.

After a few lessons of this kind, if he goes through the performance in a satisfactory manner, you can venture a little further and try him with a turn by making the motion in the wrong direction. Be very easy and go careful now, for much depends upon starting right. When all is ready wave your hand in just the opposite direction from the one that you have been accustomed to, and when he has taken two or three strides, sound the two short notes with your whistle, and at the instant he turns his head toward you, wave your hand in the other direction and proceed as in former lessons. Should he be loth to turn, you must use good judgment and get him used to it without getting him discouraged; perhaps by making him *To ho* when he refuses to turn, and then sending him in the new direction you will get safely over the difficulty. But it is seldom that you will have any trouble if you have pursued a proper course in his earlier lessons and thoroughly instilled into his mind that he must obey. We have been often surprised to see how readily our pup would at the first trial turn and take the direction indicated, thus showing that our efforts to make him feel confidence in us and that he could implicitly trust us, were crowned with success, and that instinctively as it were he obeyed the motion of our hand, although thinking that the meat was in the opposite direction.

After you once get this first turn accomplished the rest is comparatively easy, but do not hurry him as nothing is gained, and much may be lost by undue haste; and you will find that if you drill him in this until he is reasonably perfect before going any further, that when you come to try him with the second turn, he will all the more readily comprehend and obey. If at the successive steps in these lessons you are through with each one before attempting the next, you are sure to find your reward for your patient labor in the great satisfaction that you will experience when you cast him loose among the birds and witness the practical illustration of your wisdom and success as a teacher that he will be sure to afford you.

It is better to confine his beat to quite narrow limits at first, as this will keep him near you and make it easier for you to check him at once, should his performance be faulty. Three or four strides will generally be found sufficient, and in some cases even less will be found enough, and occasionally we may have a pupil whose natural aptitude for this may be indulged from the first and a still wider range allowed him; but in either case the range should be circumscribed until he appears to understand what is required, and to readily and cheerfully obey your signals and the different motions of your hand. This very important accomplishment cannot be taught in a week or a month, indeed you will do very well if you succeed in obtaining fair work out of him in a year; not but long before this time he will beat his ground in a manner that will cause even old sportsmen to pronounce him a prodigy, but as we are striving for perfection, we will not be satisfied with a mediocre performance, but continue perseveringly to practice our pupil until he will not only regularly quarter his ground in front of us and instantly obey each signal, but will wheel of his own accord when he reaches a a proper distance or comes to fence, hedge, or stream that he should not cross. This knowledge that he must not cross a fence or hedge without orders is of great importance and easily imparted by working him along a fence after he has learned to beat his ground and turn at the signal. He will, after a few lessons, understand what you desire and readily keep within bounds. Should he at any time transgress and go through or over the fence, care must be taken that he returns at once, and at the precise spot where he went through. This is of great importance, for if he is allowed to return at any other point the chances are that he will fail to realize that he has done wrong; but if you insist on his returning at the exact place, he will at once understand that something is wrong and will be more careful in the future.

While our pup is yet young he should become accustomed to the water; most young dogs will take to it readily; but should he appear to have any fear of it he must be handled with care and gradually made acquainted with it in such a manner as shall not frighten him. When he has acquired some little knowledge and you begin to take him out for a walk with you, you should visit with him some small stream or shallow pond and sit down on the bank and give him time to get acquainted with it. If he shows no inclination to wet his feet you will find it a very good plan to hold a piece of meat over the water where it is but an inch or two deep, and where he cannot get it without putting his feet in it. By carefully working him in this way he will soon learn that it will not hurt him; and in a short time he will fearlessly wade across the shallow stream with you and soon, if the right course is pursued, he will venture anywhere. You should never throw him in no matter how much you may feel disposed to do so, but rather let him find out for himself that water will not hurt him, and he will soon lose all fear.

CHAPTER VI.

RETRIEVING.

RETRIEVING is an accomplishment that nearly all sportsmen place a high value upon, and even its opponents generally become quick converts to the practice as soon as they are fortunate enough to own a dog that is well-trained in this almost indispensable branch of canine education. We have often been amused at the sudden change in the mind of some of these out-spoken adversaries of the practice upon their acquisition of a really good retriever. How quickly their fears that it will make him unsteady vanish; how soon their belief that it will ruin his nose takes flight, and henceforth the system has no stronger advocate until they get another worthless animal. We do not propose to argue the question here as to whether retrieving is detrimental to the dog or not, but will, instead, state that it is our firm belief that if our dog is properly trained in the first place, and kept up to his work as he should be, no possible harm can accrue either to his nose or steadiness; and that in no single instance where evil results have ensued was it the fault of the practice or the dog, but entirely the fault of the man; for the dog is certainly not to blame for breaking shot and chasing the wing-broken bird when his master sets the example. Neither should he be blamed for repeating the indiscretion. Here we can see that the check cord and spiked collar could be used to very great advantage, but we should by no means test its efficacy upon the neck of the dumb animal.

We will now resume our lessons, reserving further remarks upon this very important subject until we come to actual work in the field. We do not think it advisable to commence teaching our pup to retrieve until he has shed his puppy teeth, and his permanent set are pretty well grown; for until this time his mouth is generally more or less inflamed, and his first teeth are sharp as needles; and we may not hope to succeed in achieving that dainty, delicate mouth—that is so indispensable to the good retriever—as certainly as we shall if we wait until his gums are hardened and he has become somewhat accustomed to his new teeth. He will also have acquired all the more experience with the added days, and will all the more readily understand what you require. We shall now derive no little benefit from our so-called "fancy training." In fact, should our pupil possess no natural taste for retrieving, we shall find it almost indispensable; and should he prove never so hard-headed and never so hard-mouthed, we may rest assured that with the help of this same fancy training we shall be able to bring him safely through, and that no doubting fears will disturb our mind when we send him for his first bird.

Our pupil should be well up in all his lessons by this time, and so perfect at *To ho* that he will not only "draw" on a piece of meat one step at a time, but he must be also so well trained that when you cluck to him as a signal that he may eat it, he will, after taking it in his mouth instantly, at your command of *To ho*, hold it perfectly still and deliver it into your hand without any hesitancy. If this has been thoroughly taught him, one-half your task in teaching him to retrieve is accomplished, and you will find it an easy matter to complete his education; for you will have no trouble in inducing him to take a single step toward you when he has the piece of meat in his mouth; and by using great care that you do not tax his patience too much by an undue haste to perfect him too soon, he will, in a short time, readily take two or three steps, and with proper care and good judgment on your part he will soon learn to readily bring you the smallest bit of meat from across the yard, and to deliver it into your hand intact.

We must again caution you to go very slow, and to be satisfied with a very little progress. In this lesson especial care must be had that each successive step is well and thoroughly learned before proceeding any further. Thus, when you have succeeded in getting him to take a step or two toward you, do not try him at a longer distance until he has had considerable practice at this, and will readily come the step or two at the word "*bring;*" or you can use the word "*fetch*" if you prefer, but do not use more than one of them, at least until your pupil is further advanced. Of course you will have taught him to come to you when called, long before this, and by prefacing your call with the word *bring*, or *fetch*, it will not be long before he will understand its meaning; but until he does understand it and comes readily at the word you shou'd not increase the distance.

There is a great difference in dogs in learning this; some of them will give you scarcely any trouble and from the first appear to know just what you want and take delight in bringing anything you may throw for them; while others seem to be stupid and will never bring anything of their own accord. The first is a natural retriever and will be easily taught, and also easily spoiled. The last, although harder to teach, will make nearly as good a retriever as the former if the proper course is pursued. We very much dislike that a pup should retrieve before his mouth is all right and his permanent teeth well grown; for this propensity, if indulged before this time is very apt to give you a hard-mouthed dog. Hence, for this reason, we never encourage a pup to bring anything while at play. In fact he should never for a moment be allowed to think that he is at play while under instruction in any of his lessons, for there is nothing that is so conducive to bad behavior and disobedience as this. Therefore, make him realize that when you require him to do anything you mean work and not play.

Do not forget that he must never be allowed to eat the piece of meat that he has held in his mouth or brought to you, but that he must be rewarded with something different. This is a very important point, and you will find it very useful in perfecting the delicate mouth that we all admire so much. You must also insist upon instant obedience to your command to drop. This can be obtained at the outset by practice with your hand, clasping his muzzle as we have before described, and this must be resorted to should he show the slightest inclination to hesitate or roll the morsel around in his mouth; for we are aiming at perfection and must be satisfied with nothing short.

When our pupil has become so proficient in this that he will pick up a piece of meat and bring it a few steps and deliver it safe into your hand, you should take a piece of cloth and loosely wrap up the meat inside of it, and commence as in the first place by putting it in his mouth and proceeding as in your first lesson at this. He will probably understand what is required and very soon perform as well with this as he did with the bare meat; but should he not like this, you must proceed with the same painstaking perseverance that we have endeavored to impress upon your mind as being of the utmost importance, until your end is attained. You will find that a piece of old cotton cloth that is clean and about as large as your two hands will answer admirably. You should let him see you wrap it around the meat, that he may the more readily understand your object, and if he gives you any trouble you must be very careful that you do not try to force him too fast. Perhaps you will find it expedient to leave the meat partially exposed until he understands what is wanted. Or you can merely tie a shred of the cloth to it for a while, and very gradually increase the amount until you have it entirely covered. Your knowledge of his disposition will aid your judgment in so timing his lessons and in so conducting any new experiments that he shall not become disgusted nor sulky, thus giving you no end of trouble. Your aim should be to so handle him that his lessons shall prove a source of enjoyment, and he be ever anxious to receive your instructions. This you can easily accomplish by a proper system of rewards when he does well, and by lavishing upon him unstinted caresses and praise when giving his lessons. To bring about this result you may find it advantageous to be chary of your caresses at other times and to reserve your words of praise for your hours of practice; but this will be necessary only in extreme cases.

When our dog brings in his birds in the faultless manner that we have been at so much trouble to teach him, we shall want to see him deliver them into our hand in the same faultless style. And to secure that end we will teach him to come with his captive directly in front of us and to sit on his haunches with his head well up and quietly await our pleasure. Proceed to do this by calling him up in front of you, and placing one hand upon his hips and the other under his chin, gently, yet firmly, force his hind parts down while you hold up his head, at the same time telling him to "sit." This will be enough for the first lesson, and by continuing in this manner he will soon sit at the word, and then you can give him the order every time that he brings the piece of meat, taking care that he sits directly in front of you every time and remains quiet for a second or two before delivering it; and in a short time he will become so accustomed to this that he will do it of his own accord. We prefer that our dog should bring his birds in the good old-fashioned way, by taking them well into his mouth. This becomes a necessity when the bird is only wing-broken, and to our mind it is far more preferable at all times. Especially is it so when among close lying birds; for with the bird in his mouth, back away from his nose, he will not be nearly so apt to flush game that may be in his path. Still we have trained dogs to fetch the bird by one wing, which is easily done by taking half a dozen of the stiff wing feathers of any game bird, or if those cannot be had, those of a fowl will answer. These should be braded together and then sewed in place with stout pack thread. This braiding and sewing is to give him a hold with his teeth so that he will not be obliged to grip them, thus giving him a hard mouth. This should be regularly used after he has learned to bring his piece of meat. Perhaps it would be well to tie a bit of meat to it at first, and, when he will bring it readily, a small stone that will weigh two or three ounces should be attached to it, and as he improves you can gradually add to the weight until it approaches the weight of the bird, say nearly half pound. Care should be taken to make the feathers fast to the stone so that they will not come apart. We do not recommend this style, but as many think that it is quite an accomplishment, we give our method, which has proved successful. Should you wish to adopt this course you should confine your practice entirely to this bunch of feathers, and when he brings it readily you should vary the performance by attaching different articles instead of the stone—your knife, for instance, or a bunch of keys or a bit of wood, and by always making him bring by taking the feathers in his mouth, he will readily learn to bring his birds in the same manner if you show him how with a few of his first ones by placing the wing in his mouth, or perhaps the mere showing him the wing will be sufficient.

Should you decide for the old-fashioned way, you should procure a soft ball. We have found a ball of lampwicking to be the best possible thing that could be devised—it is soft and just about the right size. This should be stitched through and through, so that it will not unravel, and after he brings his bit of meat in good shape you can try him with this. You will find that the best plan to pursue is to commence at the beginning, and place it in his mouth as you did the first piece of meat, and to pursue the same course by asking only one or two steps, until he gets accustomed to it. And be sure and do not try to accomplish too much at once, but go no faster than your pupil's progress will warrant. When you think that it will answer to order him to pick it up and bring it to you, watch him very closely, and if there is going to be any trouble, and he does not seem inclined to pick it up readily, you must instantly go to him and place it in his mouth, and be content to let him bring it this way for this time, and wait until he is very hungry, and then try him by tying a piece of meat to the ball, and he will soon learn what is required and give no further trouble. When he brings his ball readily, you should procure some feathers—from the body of a game bird if possible, but those of a fowl will do very well—and commence by sewing two or three of them on the ball; and as he becomes accustomed to them you should add more until the surface is entirely covered. This will accustom him to feathers, and he will not refuse to take a bird in his mouth as we have known some dogs to do that were really good retrievers. We should not advise you to require your pupil to bring anything except bits of meat and this ball; until he does this in good form and appears to fully understand what you require. Then you should gradually accustom him to bring other articles—a half sheet of newspaper crumpled into a ball the size of your fist is a good thing to practice him on, always remembering to commence with anything new, by first carefully placing it in his mouth and requiring him to bring it but a step or two the first time. This may seem needless to you, but you will find it necessary with some dogs, and we have ever found that the best results have been obtained by strictly following this course, no matter how intelligent our pupil may be, nor how willing to bring anything that you may wish him to.

CHAPTER VI.—CONTINUED.

RETRIEVING.

SHOULD you desire that your dog become proficient in the fancy department of this accomplishment, there is no end to the tricks that you may teach him; but until he is fairly proficient in bringing his bit of meat and ball, you should confine your practice strictly to these; for although he may understand you and readily bring anything that you may ask him to, you will find it the better way to go slow and sure, ever bearing in mind that anything that is worth your while to teach him, should be taught in a thorough manner, that he may not forget it should it happen that he should go a few days without being called upon to perform it.

We like our dog to carry, as well as to fetch, and deliver his bird to our companion who has shot it; and we wish him so well trained that he will carry any article and lay it down at the word "drop" in any place that we may designate. This he may be taught to do understandingly if you pursue the proper course with him. To teach him this, you will require an assistant, who should be one of your own family, or some one that the dog is well acquainted with. When you give the first lesson, your assistant should be a few feet from you. Calling your pupil to you, give him his ball and bid him "carry" it, at the same time motioning with your hand in the direction that he is to go. Your assistant should not say a word, but should merely hold out his hand for the ball, and when the dog delivers it, he should praise and pet him a little, while you should make make much of him, and if he has performed the task in a pleasing manner, reward him with a bit of meat. After a few lessons of this kind, the distance can be gradually increased and he will soon carry as far as he can see your assistant. If there is any difficulty in getting him started right, let your assistant take the ball and send him to you, until he understands what is wanted, which he will do after a few lessons. Of course, you have told him to "drop" every time that he delivers anything to you, and as he knows the meaning of the word, it will be an easy task to teach him to lay down his ball or bit of meat in any place that you may wish him to. In order that he may learn to do this in a proper manner and readily drop his burden at the word, and instantly leave it without regret and come to you, we will commence at the beginning and give him the order for the first time when he is close to us, and with our hand extended as if to take it. As soon as he opens his mouth the hand should be instantly removed and the article allowed to drop on the ground. At once praise and pet him and give him to understand that this is all right. On no account must you pick up the article or he may be led to think that he should have delivered it into your hand as usual, nor should you allow him to pick it up, but at once call him away and interest him with something else. This will be enough for the first lesson. This should be repeated until he appears to understand what is required, before you attempt to increase the distance. Your pupil must be made to understand that when he hears the order to drop he must instantly lose his hold, and leaving the article, at once obey whatever signal you may give him. You should so teach him that when coming in with anything that you have ordered him to bring he will at the word drop it and wheel at the motion of the hand in any direction that you may indicate. You will derive no little benefit from this accomplishment should you ever get in a "hot corner" on a duck pass, and not only save yourself much worry, but also spare your dog much labor, by bidding him drop his dead bird and first secure the wounded one, which may make good its escape unless attended to at once. The same thing often occurs in quail shooting, and many birds are lost that might be brought to bag, did your dog but understand this fancy training.

The careful reader will readily understand that our so-called "fancy training" is in reality not so useless as some would-be critics would have us believe; but is a part of our system whereby we not only bring out our pupil a "killing" dog but we make of him an intelligent companion and elevate him to our own sphere, as it were, and by the wonderful development of his reasoning faculties we not only greatly increase his capacity for intelligently entering into the enjoyment of the ever changing phases of our woodland sports, but we greatly add to our own pleasure in witnessing the marvelous manifestations of reason and intelligence that he will display in his encounters with some wary patriarch of the forest, whose tricks and subterfuges will outvie the wily strategems of a Tallyrand.

There are many things that you can readily teach your pupil after you once get him fairly started on the road, for the more you teach him and the more pains you take with him the more readily will he understand what you wish. You must use great caution when you begin teaching him to bring anything that is new to him; and be very sure that he will understand your orders before you issue them. This point is worthy your careful consideration and you should strive to make yourself perfectly understood at all times. This you can easily do by closely watching his disposition and the workings of his mind as he performs his tasks. Some dogs are possessed of remarkable reasoning faculties and appear intuitively to understand just what you wish, while others are slow to learn and require more time to develop their latent powers. From personal experience we are well satisfied that the former requires to the full as much painstaking, careful handling as the latter in order to perfect his education, and make of him a steady, reliable dog. Therefore, unless you wish to see exemplified the truth of the old saying "quick learned, quick forgotten," go slow, and be very sure that every step in each lesson is well learned before you advance any further. You should never ask your dog to bring anything that will tax his powers too severely, especially should this rule be observed until his education is complete. Your judgment will tell you better than to bid him bring the crowbar or a piece of custard pie; you should likewise refrain from asking him to bring you anything that is hard or bulky, at least until he has arrived at maturity and is well established in all his lessons. Many good retrievers are ruined by allowing them to bring articles that they are obliged to grasp hard in order to hold on to. For this reason we never allow our dog to bring our knife nor anything of the kind, for just so sure as this is allowed just so sure will the dog acquire the habit of pinching his birds.

We once owned one of the best retrievers that we ever saw. In an evil hour we bade him carry into the house the earthen plate from which he had eaten his dinner. After this it became the regular thing for him to do at every meal, but alas that dainty, delicate mouth, which had been our pride and boast, was gone forever, and after this every bird that he brought that was not stone dead, would show the marks of his teeth. We are well aware that there is a great difference in dogs in this respect, and that we occasionally see one that will bring anything that he can drag along and at the same time he will hardly ruffle a feather of a struggling bird; but for fear that you may not possess such a paragon we advise you to be very careful about trying any experiments that may ruin your dog, especially when there is no practical benefit to be derived that is at all commensurate with the risk that you run. Your hat and gloves and slippers, you can safely allow him to bring you, and it will take but little time to teach him this if you carefully follow the instructions that we have given. You can even teach him by constant practice to distinguish between them so that when you send him for either one he will make no mistake, but, understanding your order, bring the article you wish. In order to teach him this you should first accustom him to bring each article and at the same time to take pains to teach him its name. Take, for instance, your hat, and after placing it in his mouth, bid him "bring the hat," and be sure to use the same language every time that you practice him at this. The same course should be pursued with the gloves or any other article that you may wish. After he has had practice enough to bring readily the article desired you can place several articles close together. Put your hat and gloves with his ball and other light articles, then order him to bring the hat, should he pick it up at the first trial, as he is very likely to do, you must praise and pet him, and as you talk to him you should speak the word "hat" in order to impress upon his memory the meaning of the word. This should be done in an intelligent manner, perhaps by saying he "is a good dog to bring the hat," just as you would talk to a boy. Should he pick up his ball, or any other article, at once tell him to "drop," and repeat the order for the hat and do not allow him to bring you anything else. After he brings the hat readily every time, you can change to something else, your gloves for instance; but until he has learned the meaning of the words and brings the articles readily, do not place the hat near them, nor where he can see it, as it may confuse him. When he has become accustomed to the gloves you can place the hat with them and he will soon understand which to bring. This course should be pursued with each article, and in a short time he will understand the meaning of the words; and when you send him for any article that you have thus taught him the name of, he will seldom make a mistake. While teaching your pupil to retrive, you should never allow yourself to become careless nor let him do this work in a slovenly manner. Always insist upon a perfect performance of his task, for if he is once allowed to depart from the accustomed manner that you have taught him he is sure to get the impression that this is right and pleasing to you, and you will have a harder task to set him right than you would to have kept him straight in the first place ; and worse than this, he will be be very liable to become confused and fail to understand just what you want; therefore, firmly insist upon implicit obedience to your ordesr, and never allow yourself to deviate one iota from the course that you have marked out.

We have ever found that all intelligent dogs are very prone to look to their masters for guidance and instinctively to take their cue from them as to their behavior. You should take every advantage of this trait, and by cool and collected behavior, under all circumstances, strive to impart to your pupil a steadiness that will ever be to you a source of pride.

This trait is especially to be cultivated when trying to make a careful, tender-mouthed retriever. You should always handle with the greatest care any article that you are teaching him to bring. There appears to be something in the careful manner in which you handle the object that is potent to impress upon his mind a corresponding carefulness in taking hold of it that is not apparent when the object is roughly thrown upon the ground; and we have frequently taken pains to go, and with ostentatious care lay the article down instead of throwing it, and have in this way succeeded in obtaining the best of results, especially when our dog was a little inclined to be rough or hard-mouthed.

There is one rule that we have carefully observed for many years, and we can assure you that it is well worthy your consideration. We never allow a pup to retrieve a bird his first season, until we have first handled it, and found that it was stone dead. You should allow him to point it for a short time and then daintily pick it up; and, after smoothing out the feathers very carefully, lay it down in front of him, taking care that he can see your every motion. Now retreat a few steps and very quietly bid him "bring dead." By pursuing this course you will improve, not only his mouth, but his steadiness as well; and also give him a chance to become acquainted with the difference in the scent between a live and a dead bird; and so render him less liable to make a mistake by pouncing upon a close-lying bird that chances to be near where he has marked the dead bird down.

Having intimated in the first chapter that we are in favor of using the whip *when it is needed*, we will briefly explain. As we have before stated we never use the whip until our pupil's education is complete, and there is no occasion to resort to it even then, unless our orders are willfully disobeyed. When we find that our pupil is willful, and deliberately refuses to perform his task, we seek occasion to give him a lesson that he will never forget. We are very careful to select an occasion for punishment when the order disobeyed is of a passive character, like *To ho* or *Charge*, as better results are obtained than when the command is of an active nature. Provided with a heavy whip, we take the opportunity when our pupil is very much engaged about something that will be pretty sure to cause him to disobey, and give him the order to *Charge*. If we are positive that he plainly understands and willfully refuses to obey, we instantly take him by the collar in such a manner that he cannot bite nor break away, and repeating the order, strike him once with all our force. Retaining our hold, we calmly wait without speaking, long enough to slowly count ten. We then repeat the order and blow simultaneously. This we continue until our judgment tells us that he has had enough. You may depend upon it that a dozen blows thus administered will accomplish more in the way of reform than a hundred thrashings as generally inflicted, for your pupil not only knows why he is punished, but he has plenty of time between the strokes to reason it all out, and he will surely come to the conclusion that you really want him to charge when you give the order; and that the best thing that he can do is to instantly obey. Unless he is uncommonly stubborn you will find that one or two such whippings will last him his lifetime. You must be very careful to issue your commands in your ordinary tone of voice; and on no account must you display the least sign of anger or impatience; and as soon as you are through with the punishment you must speak a few kindly words to him in order to let him understand that you are still his loving friend. As soon as he recovers a little, you should repeat your order, while he will at once obey, when you must pet and praise him without stint, thus indellibly impressing upon his mind that the way of the canine transgressor is hard and that obedience will bring a sure reward. We very much dislike to punish a dog; but if this has to be done, we greatly prefer that the lesson should be given before we take him into the field, as the knowledge thus imparted may prevent the necessity of resorting to this extreme when among the birds.

CHAPTER VII.

IN THE FIELD.

IN the preceding chapters all of our work has been of a preliminary character. We have expended much time and patience in order to perfect our pupil in the rudiments of the education that is so indispensable to that pride of the sportsman's heart, a good dog. Long ago we thought our pet was just about perfection in the performance of his duties and have anxiously awaited the coming of the crisp October days that we might put to the test our hopes, and, by actual trial in the field, demonstrate how much of wisdom pertains to the course that we have pursued. Do we live among the forest-crowned hills, the home of the lordly ruffed grouse; long ago we have located several broods of these regal birds, and as we have paid them an occasional visit, how our blood has warmed up, how our nerves have thrilled as we fondly dreamed of the sport in store for us when the falling leaf should proclaim that

> The hunter's glorious days have come,
> The best of all the year;
> When through the woodland shades we roam
> With royal sport to cheer.

Should our home be toward the setting sun on the broad prairie, whose vast expanse teems with numberless broods of the toothsome chicken, with ever-growing delight and satisfaction have we witnessed from day to day the added strength of the whirring pinion, and with ever-increasing impatience at laggard time's slow flight have we awaited the dawn of the auspicious day that brings such wealth of joy to the sportsman's heart. Or, perchance, our hopes of happiness are turning to the pride of the stubbles, the gamy, beautiful quail. How eagerly have we beaten the feeding grounds, and as the merry bevy, with tumultuous roar, have burst upon our sight, how have we, with throbbing pulse, watched the flitting wings, and carefully marked their flight as they settled in the friendly cover or upon the distant hillside. What visions of lithe bounding forms suddenly transformed into living statues, mingled with flashing brown sprites, the crack of the gun, and the cloud of fleecy feathers floating in air, have filled us with anticipated satisfaction, as we thought of the pleasure in store for us when the early frosts should call us forth to the field. Or do thoughts of that long-billed aristocrat of birds, "woodcock the magnificent," alone engage our thoughts. Well, we know their sure abiding place, and as we have paid them our devoir and seen them dart through the openings, and heard their querulous whistle, how have we thought that the sere and yellow leaf would soon be here to bring to us most royal sport. Do not look upon this as a digression, for we dearly love the pursuit of every one of these favorites; and we hope that you, dear reader, like ourselves, will so train your dog that, no matter where your lines are cast, your pleasant sport is sure.

Our favorite sport since childhood has been the pursuit of that best of all game birds, the magnificent ruffed grouse, and we have ever found, when our dog was anywhere near perfect in circumventing this most wily bird, that but few days, or perhaps hours, of practice were required to make him equally adept in the pursuit of any of the others. Many writers pronounce this beautiful bird unfit to train a dog upon; they rail against his subtle cunning, and are unstinted in condemning his swiftness of wing; and they will give you columns in disparagement of his preternatural wisdom, which they miscall wildness, and earnestly advise you to keep your young dog away from the ruffed grouse's haunts. Notwithstanding the evident sincerity of these writers, we must beg to differ from their views, and can only regret that their knowledge of the habits of this king of birds is not equal to their skill in framing sentences for his vilification

Having decided to give our pupil his first practical lessons with this most potent instructor as our co-worker, let us "hie away to the fields with eager dog and trusty gun," and test the sport so long anticipated. Our pupil should be kept at heel until we reach the usual haunt of the birds, when he should be encouraged to go on. Let him go where he pleases, taking care only to keep him within bounds and always under your eye, that you may see just what he is doing. Do not bother him with any orders, if you can possibly avoid it; above all, do not make him beat each particular corner that you may think desirable, but rather allow him to take the lead and to have his own sweet will, content to follow him until he has gained some little insight and become somewhat accustomed to the new life just opening before him. See with what eager pleasure he explores the hidden mysteries of the covert, how his every graceful motion tells of joy; how his sparkling eyes mirror his delight; but look, and proudly feast your eyes upon the welcome sight, he has discovered that something is in the wind and the "heaven born instinct" within has frozen him rigid as the rock by his side. Choke down that rising lump in your throat; quiet the quick throbbings of your heart; and, while blessing your good fortune, be cool and collected, for never more need of cool, deliberate action than now. Your dearest foe is near, and faltering eye or trembling hand will insure his triumphant escape and cause you unwelcome discomfiture. Do not hurry, but, with deliberate haste, walk forward and force a rise; calmly now, and, as though on parade and about to shoot at a chip tossed in air, coolly bring your gun into position, glance along the trusty barrels and, with "eye of faith and finger of instinct," "cut loose," and fortune grant your aim be true! The chances are greatly against your obtaining a close shot at the first rise, unless among young and unsophisticated birds; but shoot you must, nevertheless, even should the flashing form be far beyond your reach or, as very often happens, entirely out of sight, for we have not done with him yet; and most potent is the sound of gun and whistle of the hurtling lead to drive from his crafty brain the wisdom that causes him to shun our close acquaintance. Should your shot prove deadly and the conduct of your dog be all that you could wish, with a loving pat and kindly words, lead your pet straight to your victim and as soon as his sensitive nose locates the bird, at once pet and praise him without stint and talk to him as to an intelligent companion. After a few seconds you should pick up the bird in a dainty manner, and while carefully smoothing out the feathers, allow the dog to snuff the grateful perfume, but on no account let him mouth it, nor poke his nose among the feathers, thus teaching him that the greatest care must be taken that not a feather should be displaced.

When your pup first shows sign that he has scent, do not on any account speak to him nor make any sign, but allow him to act his own pleasure. Should he go through the trying ordeal to your satisfaction, congratulate yourself that you are possessed of a wonder; should his earnest inclination overpower his innate sense of duty and cause him to become unsteady and flush the bird, you must at once call him in and place him as near as may be in the exact position that he occupied when he should have pointed, and commanding him to *to-ho*, give him to understand that you are displeased with the performance. If you have killed the bird, and can readily find it, you will add to the force of this lesson if you oblige him to retain his position while you go and bring it to him, and as you hold it a foot or two from his nose, repeat your command of *to-ho*. This, you will find, will cause him to be more careful in the future. Should he become demoralized at the rise of the bird and give chase, do not despair, but calmly say *to-ho*, and if he disregards the command, let him go, and be thankful that he has ambition, consoling yourself with the knowledge that in a short time you can eradicate the fault, while the virtue will remain and afford you great satisfaction in the future. When he returns you should at once replace him in the position from which he broke, and make him *to-ho* for a short time, while you talk to him about the enormity of the offence. It is not advisable to shoot when he starts to chase, as should you kill, he may seize the bird and handle it too roughly for his future good. Neither does the sound of the gun exercise a steadying influence upon his excited nerves. Above all else, do not fail to keep perfectly cool yourself under all circumstances, and to issue all your commands in your ordinary tone of voice, for there is nothing so conducive to unsteadiness in your dog as his knowledge of the fact that you are demoralized, and he is sure to become possessed of this knowledge almost before it is apparent to you. Therefore earnestly strive to retain your self control, for without that you can never succeed in turning out a steady dog.

Should your bird escape the first onslaught, let no common occurrence prevent you from immediately following him up. Do not undertake this in a half hearted manner, but put your whole soul into the work and rest not until you have again routed him. Give him a shot as he rises, and if he again escapes be not discouraged, but with renewed efforts try him again, secure in the knowledge that, can you but find and keep him moving—although he may be the wisest and, consequently, the wildest grouse of them all—at last your reward is sure; at last, utterly demoralized by the relentless persistency of your pursuit, he has changed his tactics, and, quietly crouching on the ground with fear and trembling, waits for you to pass. Fatal mistake! The keen-nosed dog, more eager at each successive defeat, again becomes statuesque and unerring'y indicates the bird's hiding place. Now is the supreme moment. With nerves of steel—hardened by the excitement of the long continued chase—you literally kick him from his retreat and cooly bring him down. What satisfaction is in your heart as you smooth his beautiful plumage. What light is in your eye as you gaze upon his plump form. What pride is yours as you complacently view the noble prize so gallantly won. A glance at the speaking countenance of your four-footed friend tells you that he, too, is happy; and, our word for it, a few days among these crafty birds will do more to develope the hunting sense of an intelligent animal than thrice the time devoted to the pursuit of any other game.

CHAPTER VIII.

IN THE FIELD.

HOW rare it is to see a strictly first-class dog. Good ones we may find in abundance; but the paragon, who has no failings and all the virtues, is—although often heard of—seldom seen. Glancing back through the many years that we have ardently followed the delightful sports of the field we can call to mind but few among the many dogs that we have seen afield that come up to our standard of excellence, and those, almost without exception, received their early training among the ruffed grouse. There is something pertaining to the pursuit of these must cunning birds that is potent to sharpen the wits and develop the intelligence of your dog that you will fail to find accompanying the pursuit of any other game. It is for this reason that we endeavor to give our dog his first lessons in the field upon this bird. We are well aware that more than one writer of renown strongly condemns this best of birds as totally unfit to train a dog upon, taking the ground that they are so very difficult to bring to bag that the dog becomes discouraged. We know that the reverse of this is true, for we have given scores of youngsters their first tuition among these noble birds, and we have yet to see the one who showed the first indication of anything of the kind; on the contrary, we have ever found that—after one or two successful encounters with these most wary birds—no matter how long and unsuccessful the chase, our pupil's ardor was not checked in the least, but seemed to increase with each successive defeat.

As we have before remarked, it is better that nothing be said to your dog upon his first introduction to game, at least so long as he does nothing wrong, as this is an entirely new experience to him, and should you bother him with orders he may become confused and fail to perform nearly as well as he would if left entirely alone. Great care must be taken that he be not kept too long at work. We have ever found that the best results were obtained when we have taken our dog home after an hour or two, or even sooner, when his performance had been satisfactory. We have often taken him home at the end of a few minutes even, when everything had gone just right and we had by abundant praise and caresses impressed indellibly upon his mind that his behavior was pleasing to us, thus leaving him to ponder over the matter in a happy state of mind that would cause him to look forward with eager anticipation to future enjoyment of other blissful hours among the birds, instead of going on and, possibly, being obliged to take him off at a time when something of a disagreeable nature had occurred that would exert a depressing influence upon his susceptable mind and, perhaps, cause him to dread or, at least, to feel indifference about repeating the performance. After one or two outings, and he has become somewhat accustomed to the new experience, you can safely commence to teach him as to what he may and may not do; you can in a measure control his range and dictate as to the direction that you wish him to take, using great care that you do not restrain him too much at first, but very slowly and by easy steps gradually teach him to look to you for guidance; and if you pursue the proper course he will soon obey your lightest word as readily as when taking his regular lessons at home. This result can be obtained in this manner much sooner and much better than by trying to control him and to make him do everything just right from the start, only bear in mind that when you do order him to do anything insist upon prompt obedience every time. Among the first things that you should endeavor to instil into his mind is the knowledge that he must "work to the gun." This can be very easily accomplished if you will pursue the proper course. In the first place, under no circumstances should he be allowed to flush the birds. Not so much perhaps that it will make him unsteady, for many dogs can be taught to flush their birds to order without detracting from their steadiness, but such a course we have ever found decidedly unsteadies the wary grouse and renders them less liable to lie close than when they are walked up by the hunter. This is also the case, although in less degree, with the quail. With the woodcock we do not believe that it makes much difference, yet we would advise under all circumstances, no matter how great the temptation, your dog be not allowed to flush his bird, for many really good dogs are ruined by this practice, besides, as a rule, the more killing, as well as sportsmanlike way, is to walk up your bird. This practice you will find will soon make you a better shot than you can ever hope to be if you constantly keep in the openings and trust to the chances there to be obtained. Your dog will also improve much faster if you pursue this course, for he will instinctively realize that you are with him body and soul, and consequently he will put forth his best efforts and soon learn the grand secret of "working to the gun." This very valuable trait is rarely found in a dog unless the gun has first set the example by working to him. Ponder this well and try to realize what the thoughts of your dog must be when you leave him on his point and, sneaking off to one side, or perhaps to his rear out of sight, bid him put up the bird which he knows full well by experience will fly into the cover instead of out. We always require our dog while young to staunchly hold his point until ordered on. He will easily learn to do this if you steady him a few times and do not allow him to stir until you are beside him. This, if rightly managed, will prove a very killing trait, but unless the proper course is pursued your dog is apt to acquire the very bad habit of making false points. Great good judgment is required to so conduct his training in this that it may prove a source of pleasure instead of disappointment. Your knowledge of his disposition will aid you in adopting the right course to accomplish the desired result.

As soon as you observe that he has scent command him to *To ho*, and keep him on point until you are nearly beside him, when, without stopping, you must cluck to him to go on, accompanying the cluck with a wave of the hand, and walk just behind him until he again stops. Should he be unwilling to move on at your first order, you must not stop, neither should you pass by him, but keep stepping, even if you have to put your feet in the same place, and again cluck, or perhaps you may have to speak to him. Should he still remain staunch, the chances are that the scent is strong, and that the game may be close by, in which case you should advance and flush the bird, and, if the conduct of your dog has been irreproachable, kill if you can, but on no account must you shoot unless his behavior has been all that you could wish; for one of the most important lessons to impress upon his mind is that, just so surely as he does not perform his part in a proper manner, just so surely no birds will be the result. Do not forget, if his performance has been worthy, to pet and praise him, while, on the other hand, if no bird has been found, you should return behind him and order him on, and let him know that this is not the proper way, but that he must move on until he is near the bird. This is rather a delicate matter, and often requires nice discrimination to determine just what to do, for there is not a second to be lost in deliberation, and instant action should be taken; for if you hesitate your dog may become addicted to making false points or pottering, and, rather than this, it will be far better to score an occasional flush. Should he flush a bird by moving up, even if you have ordered him on, you must instantly check him, and bring him back to the place where he should have remained staunch, and keep him at *To ho* a short time, while you chide him for the offence. After a few lessons of this kind —perhaps, even, on the second occasion—you should order him on a little before you reach his side, and at each succeeding time you should do this still further away, until he will, at the motion of the hand, move on when you are at quite a distance from him. If he is possessed of a reasonable amount of intelligence, and you pursue the proper course, he will soon understand just what you wish, and always stop at the first indication of scent and look at you for the signal to go on, instead of following up the trail, perhaps out of your sight, and oftentimes causing you no end of trouble to find him. He will also soon learn to move on of his own accord when the scent is not just to suit, provided he knows that you can see him and are coming his way. This accomplishment is invaluable when shooting in thick covert, or beating the snipe meadows, while it can work no possible harm either on the prairie or stubble. Of course, we cannot give instructions that will cover every case, as there are so many different circumstances connected with the events of a single day, and the dispositions of the different animals are also so widely dissimilar that it is impossible for us to give anything more than a general outline of the course to be pursued. We take it for granted that the reader of ordinary intelligence who has followed us thus far has gained some idea of our system, and that his own good sense, coupled with the intimate knowledge that he must possess of the disposition and intelligence of his pupil, will safely tide him over any minor difficulties that may occur.

CHAPTER IX.

WORKING IN COMPANY.

IN the previous chapters we have carefully refrained from saying anything about the great benefit to be derived from having a trained dog to assist you in perfecting your pupil in his lessons. We have purposely pursued this course in order to show the new beginner that he can safely rely upon his own resources, and surely bring his pupil through all right, without any assistance. Nevertheless we have ever found that an old dog that is well trained and steady is of great importance in perfecting the pupil in the rudiments as well as the higher branches of his education; and we cannot forbear devoting a little space to the subject. In the first place our canine co-worker should be thoroughly trained and quick to obey; he must also be very intelligent and and of a good disposition. You should let the two associate together from the first, and they will soon become attached to one another, unless the old dog is unusually surly. We do not recommend that the pup should receive any guidance from the old dog until he is sufficiently grounded in his lessons to understand what is required of him. Thus, in teaching him *To ho*, after he will go through the performance fairly, we take the old dog into the pen with him, and after they have had a little time at play we take the pup in our arms, and making sure that he sees all that is going on, we place two pieces of meat on the ground about two feet apart, and, calling up the old dog, make him, at the word *To ho*, point one of the pieces. We then walk around a little, with the pup still in our arms, taking care that he can see the performance all the time. We then place the pup with his nose within a few inches of the second piece, and telling him to *To ho*, make him wait a few seconds, and then cluck as a signal that they can each eat their piece. This has a wonderfully steadying effect upon the pup, especially

WORKING IN COMPANY.

when you come to prolong the time a little, for he, seeing that the old dog is perfectly staunch and steady, will soon learn to emulate him. He will also acquire the very important habit of remaining steady when in the company of other dogs; this we consider of great importance, and under all circumstances we accustom the pup to doing his work in the presence of his companions, even if we have to impress the services of a cur and chain him in one corner of the pen. If this latter course has to be adopted, it is not necessary that it should be commenced until our pupil is somewhat advanced in his education, as the only object in view is to accustom him to perform his duties in the presence of other dogs, and to lay the ground work of that steadiness when among strangers that is so pleasing to see. So particular are we in this, that we invariably train our pup to point a piece of meat and stand perfectly staunch, while his companion takes the bit and eats it. This he will readily learn to do if you immediately reward him with another piece. If he is well trained in this he will not annoy you by going to pieces should half a dozen dogs rush in upon the bird that he is pointing.

After our pup is well acquainted with the old dog and has become accustomed to the chain, they should be coupled together for a short time each day until he gets used to it. We shall find further on that this will be a great help to us. The coupling chain should be short with two good swivels. Most persons make a mistake in having the coupling chain too long. Four inches is plenty long enough when your dogs are anywhere near of a size, and you will generally find it long enough under any circumstances. Should the old dog be very high headed the chain can easily be lengthened an inch or two. After they go well together and our pupil has learned the meaning of *To ho* and minds fairly, you will find that it will be of great benefit to him to practice him when coupled to the old dog, for the example of the latter will steady him, which is a matter of great importance, and once his mind is thoroughly impressed with the idea that he must hold his position, even when in fear that his companion will secure the tempting morsal, it will be comparatively easy to keep him up to his work. He will also learn to remain quiet at charge with much less trouble to you if coupled to the old dog. As he grows older and you commence to lengthen the time that he must remain in this position, we should by all means recommend this course; indeed we have found that the services of a well trained, steady dog are invaluable all through until our pupil's education is complete. As we have before remarked the assistance of the old dog should never be called in requisition until our pupil has been taught his lesson and is somewhat proficient in its performance, then he can understandingly view the old dog as he performs the task, and if he is reasonably intelligent he will soon learn to imitate his steadiness.

We shall also find, if our pup is inclined to work too close to us when quartering his ground, that the example of the old dog will soon cause him to increase his range. We much prefer that our pup should range freely of his own accord, but should he not quite please us in this, we couple him to the old dog and practice them together until we obtain satisfactory results. Great caution must be observed in this and the lessons must not be too frequent nor too long continued, or our pupil will lose his independence and form the very bad habit of looking to his companion to cut out the work which will seriously detract from his usefulness in the field.

As it is very desirable that our dog should possess a fair amount of speed, we should so conduct his exercise that when we come to cut him loose in the field he will not potter and poke, but at once strike a slashing gait and with head well up, take to his work like a veteran. Many dogs can never become fast, but if you have followed the instructions in selecting your pup that we have laid down, and have secured a well formed one with plenty of life and spirit, there will be no trouble in bringing him out a fairly speedy animal; indeed, we have taken in hand old dogs that were decidedly slow, and in a few weeks, by judicious management, have succeeded in turning them out astonishingly fast. Of course, we cannot give instructions that will enable you to infallibly produce a speedy animal, but if you will intelligently follow our plan, you can in most cases succeed in accomplishing your purpose. Do not forget, in your anxiety for speed, that a fast dog with a slow nose is nearly worthless; therefore, before you attempt to force the pace, you should thoroughly satisfy yourself that your pupil's olfactory organs are all right; you can form a nearly correct opinion upon this point by carefully watching him while he is at play, and taking note of each time that he "winds" anything that attracts him, and paying close attention to the distance he is from the object. This, though not an infallible test, will generally give you a very good idea of his powers. Should he appear to have a quick sensitive nose and you desire to quicken his gait, try the following plan, and our word for it, if you pursue the proper course, you will be astonished at the improvement he will show in a few lessons. When commencing these lessons you should select for exercise ground a large open field, and if the surface is undulating, it will be all the better, for when the old dog disappears over the knolls it will make the pup all the more eager to join him. When you arrive at the ground you should let the old dog go, and keep the pup close at heel until he gets quite impatient, taking great care not to overdo the matter by keeping him under restraint too long, nor on the other hand should you let him go until he is in the proper frame of mind to put forth his best efforts when he hears the welcome signal. If you have acquired such knowledge of his disposition and temper as you should have done, you will be sure, by closely watching him, to hit upon just the right instant when his impatient feelings are at their greatest height to give him the word to go on. If this order is given in an eager tone, accompanied with a quick step or two forward, you will find that your pupil will at once start with an eager rush and put forth his best efforts to catch the old dog. You should carefully watch him, and as soon as he slacks his speed, call him in at once and keep him at heel until he is again impatient, when you can repeat the performance. If this course is understandingly pursued, your pupil will soon learn that in order to have his liberty he must not potter, and he will in a short time astonish you with his greatly improved gait. The speed of almost any dog can be improved in this way, but the best results are obtained when your dog is possessed of a high strung nervous temperament. With such a one properly handled marvelous improvement is sure to follow.

You will also find that the example of the old dog will be productive of much good, when you commence accustoming your pup to the sights and sounds of the street, you will be spared much trouble in way-wising him by coupling them together when taking a walk through the streets, especially if you are in a city where each sight and sound is new to your pupil, for he will not only see that his companion is unconcerned and thereby acquire confidence, but he will soon learn that he cannot bolt should anything strange occur, and in a short time he will become steady and behave like a veteran.

Backing is an accomplishment that affords us much pleasure—in fact, one-half of our enjoyment, when shooting over a brace of dogs, is in witnessing the faultless performance of a well-trained animal, as he instantly honors the point of his companion. This accomplishment is inherent in many dogs, and is as natural to them as the instinct of pointing. Yet, there are many first-class animals who will not back a companion's point, but will work forward until they obtain the scent. This is always unpleasant, and often not only mars our enjoyment of the sport, but the practice is very apt to unsteady the other dog, especially when the dog that should back thrusts his nose a little ahead, which he is very prone to do. The dog that will remain perfectly steady and staunch while his companion repeatedly practices this, is, indeed, a treasure, and worthy fairer treatment. That your dog will not be the one to commit so serious a fault you can rest assured, if you have carefully followed our instructions in his early training and will intelligently handle him when he first goes into the field with a companion. As we have often remarked, first impressions play a very important part in the future behavior of your dog, therefore you should be very careful that nothing occurs that will give him any wrong ideas. The first time that you take him out with another dog, they should be well acquainted, if possible, or at least have time to play together until they become somewhat used to each other. You should be accompanied by a friend, who should have the care of the other dog, while you keep your pupil close to heel until the other dog finds and comes to a point. Be very careful now, and as soon as your dog catches sight of him, raise your hand and bid him *To ho*, and on no account must you stir so much as a finger, but remain perfectly quiet and staunch, as though you were also backing, until your companion has flushed the bird. Your example will have much to do in perfecting his steadiness, and you will find that after a few lessons of this kind—even should he possess no natural inclination to back—he will understand what is required, and instantly back of his own accord as soon as he catches sight of a companion's point.

CHAPTER X.
CONCLUSION.

WE have given in the preceding chapters, as well as we were able, the outlines of the course that for more than a quarter of a century we have successfully pursued in preparing our dogs for lives of usefulness, and we believe, yes, we know, that if any one—we care not how wedded he may be to the force system—will but give our method a fair trial, henceforth the whip and check cord will form no part of his kennel appurtenances, for not alone does our system exercise an ennobling influence upon our pupil, thus making him much better qualified to become our companion, but the better, finer feelings of our own nature are not blunted and brutalized by the cruel associations necessarily present when the lash is applied to the shrinking form, nor is our enjoyment of the pleasures of the field marred by constantly recurring struggles with the sharer of our sport, who should be our obedient as well as loving friend. As the Hon. George Ashmun once remarked to us: "The humane system and the force system both accomplish the result of bringing man and dog toward the same plane, the one by elevating the brute, the other by lowering the humane creature."

In all our lessons we have endeavored to impress upon the reader the great importance of carefully studying the disposition of his pupil in order that he might intelligently apply their teachings. We have also tried to show the paramount necessity of a very cautious advance at each successive step. Yet so very important a matter do we deem this that we cannot forbear again calling your attention to it, and again cautioning you to use the utmost care in all your lessons, and to so manage that your dog shall not become overtrained, for this, although quite common, is a very serious fault, and one that will require a long time to overcome, if, indeed, you can ever quite eradicate it; and in order to secure that cheerful, willing obedience that is so desirable, it will be far better that you should devote plenty of time to

CONCLUSION.

the proper development of your pupil than by undue haste to bring him out only partially trained or cowed and disheartened by a too close or too long continued drilling at tasks that should be his delight instead of dread. In perfecting our pupil in his work in the field, great care must be taken that he always peforms his task in a faultless manner, and no thought of present enjoyment should allow you for an instant to relax that constant surveillance and watchful care that you have bestowed upon him while practicing him at home. There is no more prolific cause of the unsteadiness and disobedience exhibited by so many of the dogs we meet as the overlooking of the little faults that scarcely appear worth noticing. As we have before remarked, anything that is worth the doing is worth doing well, and in nothing is this more apparent than in the education of your dog. We don't mean by this that you should be constantly nagging him and breaking his heart with an incessant repitition of commands, but that when you do give an order you should see to it that it is at once obeyed, and to the very letter.

Especially should he be restrained from manifesting any unsteadiness or uneasiness, when in the presence of crippled birds. This can only be accomplished by a faithful adherence upon your part to the rules that you have established to govern his conduct and by a religious setting of the example that you wish him to follow, as any excitement upon your part or undue haste to secure the bird is sure to be impressed upon his susceptible mind and cause you no end of trouble in the future. Better by far that you should lose a dozen birds than that your dog should become unsteady. When it is possible, we always shoot a cripple before our young dog, and we have ever found that this course, especially when he could see the performance, exercised a steadying influence upon him, and also taught him to love and have confidence in the gun. After sufficient experience in the field, and when your dog appears to understand just what you require of him, he may safely be allowed to capture the fluttering bird, with no fear that it will cause him to become unsteady or depart from the teachings of his early days, for the course that we have pursued has wonderfully developed his reasoning faculties, and there will be no trouble in easily teaching him to comprehend that when ordered to retrieve a crippled bird, no license is thereby granted him to indiscrimately rush for every one that starts. When once we have our dog under the perfect control that it has been our aim to achieve, it is comparatively an easy matter to keep him up to his work, as our knowledge of his disposition and his knowledge of our method will render an occasional word all that will be required.

Having brought teacher and pupil safely afield, we shall now regretfully take our leave of them, trusting that not entirely in vain have been our labors, and that some at least of the new recruits to the vast army of sportsmen may be induced to follow the course here marked out, and by their success encourage others to try our humane system of training.

Upon carefully reviewing our very pleasant task, we are painfully impressed with its many shortcomings and imperfections; the most serious of these is the failure to express the ideas that we wish to convey in a satisfactory manner. Although to the best of our ability have we endeavored to impart the knowledge gained by a large experience, yet we feel that we have but crudely and imperfectly accomplished our purpose. There appears to be an indescribable, intangible something lacking which our pen is unable to portray

There is a mysterious and subtle power, inherent in some and only gained by others with long experience, that enables its possessor to exact an instant and willing obedience from the lower animals by a single word or look that others cannot compel by vociferous commands or even by blows. We have always noticed that those who possessed this peculiar gift appeared intuitively, as it were, to understand the nature and disposition of the animals under their care, and that there was invariably an almost electrical and harmonious sympathy between them. Would that we could reveal the secret of this mysterious power; then could we lay aside our pen with pride in the belief that we had laid at the feet of the sportsmen's shrine a worthy offering.

THE ONE-EYED GROUSE OF MAPLE RUN.

SOME years ago we penned the following article, which we reproduce here in order to give our readers some idea of the pleasures and perils which so endear to us the pursuit of "that best of all game birds, the lordly Ruffed Grouse."

First let me describe the locality where these incidents transpired, that you may the better understand some of the evolutions that I shall endeavor to explain. I feel entirely competent to give a description of the run, as even now, after the lapse of thirteen years, every rock, tree and shrub; every bubbling spring, each turn and twist of the little brook, even to its every merry dimple and minature cascade with its gleesome music, is so indelibly engraved upon the tablets of my memory, that I have only to mount the wings of thought, and the entire scene in all its loveliness is before me. Here, at the extreme upper end, is a gigantic rock maple, whose leaves on this golden October day are gorgeous in their bright array. Just at its foot a silvery spring gushes forth, whose sparkling waters are quaffed by many a weary one, as the well-worn path and smooth, white rock at its side attest. This fountain is the commencement of the little brook that I mentioned. For the first quarter mile of its course there is an occasional young maple, while upon each side, for four or five rods, beautiful ferns invite the shy woodcock to their grateful shade. For the next twenty yards, there is an abrupt fall of as many feet, whose steep sides are covered with an almost impenetrable growth of witch-hazel, which is now in bloom—notice the pleasing contrast between those sprays of lemon colored blossoms and the dark green of that hemlock that towers in a perfect cone, thirty feet above them—mark well this same hemlock—for under its umbrageous branches, a dastardly deed was attempted that recoiled upon the would-be perpetrator in a manner that afforded us heartfelt satisfaction. I will resume the tale farther on. At the foot of the fall, and for nearly a mile in length—by a quarter to half a mile in breadth—the ground is nearly level and covered with a rank growth of alders, growing in bunches, a few feet apart, between them the grass is green the whole year round. This lovely spot is appropriately called "Woodcock's Delight." What thrilling emotions fill my heart as, in fancy, I gaze upon its many mazy aisles. It seems but yesterday that I, a happy youth, was rambling through these silent shades; what delicious, glorious hours were these, what blessed communings with the God of Nature, prized by me far more than the famous bags of woodcock and grouse that I nearly always obtain here. The scene remains the same; but, alas! my beautiful friend of the querulous whistle is gone, I fear forever, slain by the ruthless hand of him who should protect, instead of destroy. Slain by him who, disguised as a sportsman, steals in mid-summer upon the callow brood, and murders, ay! *murders* every one; murders the enfeebled and often sick mother-bird and her unfledged chicks. May the curse of all true sportsmen rest upon you! The wrath of the hunter's God already abideth with you, for he suffers not his beautiful charges to roam in the places you have desecrated and laid waste. Excuse this digression, as my heart is broken with the utter desolation that abounds. Down a gradual descent of a few yards, covered with a dense growth of hazel, below the beautiful spot that I have just described, we come to a similar piece of ground of some twenty acres in extent, that is fl wed in winter and spring, to furnish motive power for a rickety old sawmill. There are no trees nor brush, except a fringe of willows a few yards in width entirely around the edge of the now dry pond. Below the mill a rocky gorge, grown up with hemlock, leads us down a descent for a hundred yards or more, when we come to a level open meadow, bordered upon one side by a splendid grove of magnificent white oats that covers full fifty acres. Across the meadows and two hundred yards away there is a tangled thicket of scrub-oak, overgrown with briers. At the lower side of both grove and thicket sunny knolls, partially covered with birches, trend obliquely down stream, meeting on the banks of the brook some five hundred yards below. From here to the river, about a mile away, there is a beautiful cover, nearly a mile in width, of alders and birches, with an occasional maple and walnut tree. This cover ends on the bank of the river, in a narrow grove of immense hemlocks. Trusting that you will retain enough of my rather tedious description to follow us through our ardous and long-winded chase, we will shoulder our guns and start for Maple Run. But first allow me to introduce you to my companion—old Tom Rood, as thorough a sportsman as it has ever fallen to my lot to encounter—a perfect gentleman, a first-rate shot and well skilled in all that pertains to woodcraft. Tom is possessed of an abundance of this world's goods, and spends most of his time in the forest, as his nut-brown phiz and wiry frame attest. When he is not shooting or fishing he is abroad communing with nature. There is a vein of poetry and also a slight tinge of superstition in his make-up that, with his overflowing cheerfulness, make him one of the most entertaining companions that I have ever met. Our present trip originated with him, as he had the day before, while resting on the bank of the river, at the mouth of the brook, seen, to use his words, a "spectre partridge" (ruffed grouse). While lying at full length on the grass, this bird had flown across the river and alighted within a few feet of him. As he looked up, at the slight noise she made, she walked up within two yards of his head. Examining her closely, he discovered that on the side toward him her eye was gone. Just as he had noticed this, she turned her head, and Tom solemnly averred that her good eye was as large as that of an ox; and far more brilliant than the purest diamond, her feathers were of a pale cream color, her ruff was light cherry, as was the band across her tail. Taking this in at a glance, and wishing to secure so unique a specimen, he reached for his gun, when this spectre bird slowly sank into the ground, and Tom, awe-struck, left the uncanny spot and started for home. When nearly a hundred yards away, he heard a roar that caused him to look back, and there was the spirit, going like a streak, up the run. You should have heard Tom tell the story, and have seen the weird look in his eyes as he described the scene. Always on hand when sport was to be had, I readily joined him, as, undoubtedly, this was a wary old bird, that would show us some fun. We soon arrived at the place where he had seen her last, and commenced a chase, the like of which I never expect to see again. We little thought, when we started the dogs, that beautiful morning, and gaily followed them, so full of life and hope, our exuberant spirits welling forth in lively joke and quick repartee, that evening's shade would find us a weary, used-up pair, wending our way homeward with halting steps, and no word of cheer to lighten the path. I will not anticipate, but try and be calm while I recount the story of our sorrow. Our dogs, Start and Stop, soon found a trail, and taking our usual places—Tom on their right flank and I on the left—we slowly moved on, up the run. The scent soon became hot, and the dogs refused to advance another step. We went ahead to raise the bird, and had gone some distance beyond the dogs, when, with a thunderous roar close to my ears, this spook of a bird rose behind me. I whirled around and catching my foot in something, down I went full length, and as it is my practice to shoot when a bird rises near enough, my gun went off just as I struck the ground, happily without doing any damage. "First knock-down for the spectre," cried Tom, who appeared to enjoy the sport even more than I did. As he had caught a glimpse of the bird, and was sure that it was the one we were looking for, we turned short to the left and followed on her course, which led toward the upper corner of the cover. The dogs soon struck her trail and worked it up nearly to the corner, and came to a full stop. Tom, being the nearest, went on the outside, and I walked toward him, expecting of course that one of us would get a sure shot. I could not raise the bird, and went back to the dogs, and at the word, they moved on up to the wall, and came to a point at a hole that led through to the other side. I got them over the wall, and they roaded her several rods in the open lot a few feet from the wall. I was in the cover opposite them, and was suddenly startled by a loud cry of "mark" from Tom, accompanied by a few forcible words, expressive of his disgust. I heard no rise and went over to him to see what it all meant, when he explained that the bird had risen some twenty rods away without making the slightest noise, and flown down on the outside as far as he could see. We were both of us beginning to get interested, and followed on in pretty good order, considering that we had been ou'generaled at every turn. The dogs, after considerable work, found her trail in the open lot, and followed it some distance, when we saw her rise a long way ahead; and swing to the left for a birch knoll that I have already described as leading up to a scrub oak and brier cover. She was not near enough for me to see very distinctly, but I could readily see that she was of a very light color. Sending Tom ahead to cut her off, should she attempt to make for the briers, I took the dogs and beat up the knoll, and soon had a beautiful point from Start that was handsomely backed by Stop. I knew by the eager way old Start's jaws were quivering that the bird was close by, and, stepping in ahead of him, was disgusted at seeing nothing but an ordinary grouse flounder up and make off; but as the rulling passion was ever strong, I pocketed my chagrin, and drawing a bead on him, brought him down. At the report of the gun our one-eyed friend rose twenty rods away, and knowing that it was sure death to attempt the briers, flew across the open meadows and went for the white oak grove, and I lost sight of her among the tops of the tallest trees. In vain we beat the whole cover in that direction, we could get no trace of her. Concluding that she had "treed," we commenced thumping each tree in the vicinity where I had seen her last, and soon routed her. She pitched down from the top of a tall tree like a rocket reversed, and not until within two or three feet of the ground did she alter her course. She received our fire with a cool complacency that was not shared by us, and skimming along close to the ground across the meadow, we saw her swing into the hated brier cover. Ordinarily we did not beat this cover, as it was not only terribly thick, but the briers were fearful. But we were after this bird, "with all that this implies," and did not stop to count the cost; but, after taking a few moments' rest, and eating our lunch, boldly faced the music, and were soon forcing our way through the tangled mass. The dogs soon found her trail and commenced roading, and for more than an hour we followed this goblin bird before we could force her to rise, which she finally did quite unexpectedly close by Tom, and just as he had stooped and was forcing his way through a particularly bad bunch of briers. He gamely struggled to an upright position and delivered his fire, but could not tell whether both eyes were open or shut; as, when he commenced to straighten up, a brier caught him just under his right eye, and plowed a ghastly furrow across his face, and half cut off the lower portion of his ear. When I joined him I could not forbear saying:

"First blood for the spectre."

A grim smile lit up one side of his face—the other side was covered with gore, and I was doubtful if he greeted my pleasantry with more than half a smile. As our bird had flown straight for the mouth of the rocky gully, we soon came to water, and after binding up our wounded as well as we could, we once more "returned to the charge." Toiling up the steep and slippery ascent, we flushed her from behind a rock, which she kept between her and us until well out of shot. Thinking that she would keep on as far as the hazel gully, we made a detour to avoid the terrible ascent, and skirted the edge until we came to the old mill, when, each taking a side of the pond and beating the fringe of willows, came together at the head of the pond. We hunted up the hazel gully, and over a large portion of alder cover, bringing to bag several grouse and woodcock, but saw no sign of our especial friend. On our return, we met a man who said that he had just started a white partridge from the wheel-pit of the old mill, and it had gone down the run. Although nearly night, with one accord, and without a word, we both wheeled and headed down the gorge. When near the lower end the dogs came to a staunch point. Thinking that the bird would go for the briers again, I clambered up the side, and had just reached the top, when this fiendish bird, with a malignity of purpose that I have never seen equaled, started and flew straight for my head. Tom could not see me, but I saw him raise his gun and I threw myself flat on the ground, just in time to catch half a dozen pellets. I had supposed that he was shooting fine shot, but was now ready to make oath that each one was bigger than a pumpkin. The bird was unharmed, and flew directly over me. She did not see me until within four feet of my head, and I shall never forget the scared expression of that bird's countenance. The tuft on her head rose right up like the clown's hair in the pantomime, and, convulsively beating the air with her wings, she, knowing what to expect, cringed and quivered in mortal fear. Springing to my feet, I deliberately sighted her across the barrels and pulled the trigger. No report followed, and, upon examining for the cause, I found the main spring broken. I must confess that things looked a little shaky, and I was almost persuaded that we were, as Tom now insisted, pursuing a myth. It was now sunset, and, crest-fallen and weary, we turned our faces toward home. The only words spoken by either of us were a mutual good-night, when we parted at the fork of the road, that led to Tom's house. We even forgot that we had any birds, and omitted our usual quarrel, of each trying to make the other take the game. Sadly I traversed the short distance home, and letting Start into the kitchen where I knew that he would be well cared for, I silently stole up to my room and went supperless to bed.

I was up betimes the next morning, and after an early breakfast, shouldered my spare gun, whistled for Start, and took the road for Maple Run, firmly resolved to bring home that bird or perish in the attempt. When I came in sight of the fork of the road, there stood Tom leaning on his gun waiting for me. "I knew that you would be here," said he, "although nothing was said about it, for the manner and tone which you rai l good night assured me that your heart was in the right place, and that you had enlisted for the war." We made straight for the oak grove, and crossed the meadow at the foot of the gorge, and climbing the bank to where I had last seen her, took her course and entered the briers. We found plenty of birds, and had kill d several before we found the trail of cur slippery friend. At last the dog struck a trail that led straight away for a long distance, and we rightly conjectured that we were now on the right track. With every nerve at its utmost tension, our guns tightly grasped, and eye and ear strained to catch the first signal of her presence, we carefully picked our way through the briers until we came within a few rods of the lower right hand corner. Leaving Tom with the dogs I retraced my steps a short distance, and noislessly crawled to the edge, and taking a position twenty yards out in the open, silently advanced toward the corner, and had reached within fair gun-shot of it, and was congratulating myself that I had her sure, when, hearing a slight noise at my right, I turned, and, just out of shot, saw this confounded bird silent as a ghost, flitting away straight out into the open. I watched her a long distance and saw her alight on the top of a stone-wall. I called Tom and explained the situation to him, and was much amused to see the wild, half-scared expression of his eyes as he said:

"We will stick to her as long as she has a feather left, but I know it is of no use, she will half kill us with her tom-foolery, and finally vanish in a cloud of smoke."

I added: "Or sink into the ground again."

This shot had its desired effect, and, after a brief look at the situation, we decided that I should go so far around that she could not see me, and get between her and the cover near the river that she would undoubtedly make for, while Tom was by a flank movement to send her to me, and after I had killed her we were going back into the briers, to attend to a number of birds that we had started there. I went around, and carefully keeping out of sight behind a favoring knoll, I reached the wall some three or four hundred yards below her, and crawling behind a rock, laid down and peered over the top of it, obtaining a good view of the whole performance. Tom by this time had obtained an offing, and was bearing down straight for her. When within a hundred yards of her, he commenced singing at the top of his voice, that well-known hymn:

"On Jordan's stormy banks I stand,"

and, as the wind was right, I could distinguish every word, and was thoroughly enjoying the music, as Tom was gifted with a grand voice, when I saw him suddenly bring his gun to his shoulder, and then, with a half turn, he went down all in a heap. Knowing that the bird had started, I strained my eyes to get sight of her. I soon saw her just over the wall coming straight for me. Waiting until she was within shot, and, knowing that I had a dead sure thing on her this time, I sprang to my feet, and, facing the way she was going, brought my gun to my shoulder and coolly waited until she should get past me. Glancing in her direction, I was thunderstruck to find that she was nowhere to be seen. A strange unearthly feeling of awe crept over me, my hair commenced to rise, my knees knocked together and I felt that I was indeed in the presence of something supernatural. This feeling lasted but a second or two, as, upon looking down the wall, I saw this phantom, a hundred yards away, rise from under its protecting shelter and disappear over the top of the alders. Feeling that I was deeply wronged, I sadly turned toward Tom for sympathy, and was surprised to see him sitting on the ground and beckoning for me to come to him. When I got there I found that he had sprained his ankle so badly that he was unable to stand. With shamefacedness and many expressions of heartfelt sorrow that he should have so far forgotten himself as to even think of so unsportsmanlike an act, Tom confessed that the singing was to charm the bird so that he could get near enough to shoot her before she started. Just as he raised his gun to fire, one foot went into a hole and, said he, "I received the reward justly my due."

As we were near the highway, I went over there and had to wait but a few minutes when a team came along. We took down the fences and soon had Tom safe in the wagon. Although he was suffering excrutiating torture, I never saw him more cheerful. Joke and story came from his lips in a continual stream, and he kept us in a roar all the way home. We got him in the house and, after bathing his foot in hot water and seeing him comfortable, I turned to go, when he said:

"I shall have to ride to-morrow and you had better come here and ride over with me."

Supposing that he was joking, I took my leave. The next morning I got an early start and went to his house to see how he was. I was greatly surprised to find his team at the door and to see him hobbing down the steps, using his gun as a cane, crying as he saw me:

"Come on! I had a vision last night and feel that this day will witness the humiliation of our ghostly friend, notwithstanding your superstitious belief in her invulnerability."

Thinking that his grit was of the "real old sort," I helped him get in the wagon. We drove to the saw-mill, and, leaving Tom in the wagon, where he could command the approaches, I took the dogs and started down the run. I had gone but a short distance when I met a man who said he had started a white partridge several times without getting a shot, and that she had gone up the run, and was probably in the big alder cover. I explained the situation to him, and, joining our forces, we prepared to move on the enemy's works once more. Going back to Tom, we sent him round to the lower end of the cover, while we beat up the fringe of willows and the hazel thicket. When Tom arrived at his post we heard him shout, and when we came up learned that he had started her close to the edge, and that her course was still onward and upward. Sending Tom to the upper end beyond the big hemlock, to a knoll, where he could overlook the whole ground, we separated a few rods and beat up toward him. We had gone half way up before we found her trail. I soon heard her rise some distance ahead, and saw her as she came up over the alders, make straight for the hemlock, and alight in its branches. A moment later our ears were saluted with the heavy report of a gun from under the tree, followed by a prolonged succession of unearthly shrieks and yells, that made my hair fairly rise. Knowing that some one was in serious trouble, we started upon a run to see what was the matter. I had gone but a few steps when I caught a glimpse of a ghostly streak passing overhead. Throwing my gun well ahead of it, I pulled the trigger, and was overjoyed to hear that welcome sound so dear to the sportsman's heart—a gentle thud as she struck the ground. With quickening pulse I listened to the convulsive flutter with which our gallant spirit-bird gave up her ghost. I did not go back for her, but hastened in the direction of those blood-curdling yells that did not cease until we struggled through the thicket into the open space under the hemlock, where we found an overgrown lout of a boy hanging head downward on the slippery ledge, with one foot caught in a crevice of the rock. We released him unharmed, and went up the bank into the open where we found Tom holding his sides and laughing like one possessed. As soon as we came to him he turned with flashing eyes upon the culprit, and, shaking his long, bony finger at him, exclaimed:

"Served you right—shoot at a poor defenseless partridge up a tree, will you? The next time you cut such a caper I hope——"

"That you will sprain your ankle," added I, to the evident discomfiture of Tom.

At this juncture old Start made his appearance with the bird in his mouth. When Tom saw her he exclaimed—and sticks to it to this day—that the dog caught her—and that none of us were smart enough to ruffle a single one of her beautiful feathers. SHADOW.

MY OLD DOG TRIM.

IT is with mingled feelings of pleasure and regret that I take up my pen to write the biography of my old dog Trim, alas! long since translated to the happy hunting grounds. Peace be with him, and may his future be as pleasant as the days spent on earth. May he find in those spirit woodlands numberless ruffed grouse, and obtain for a companion some congenial human spirit to roam with him their grateful shade until I shall come. Then will his cup of happiness ever overflow, and the reward so well earned here be his.

Trim was rather an ordinary looking-pointer, of the old Spanish type. His sire came from Cuba, and was said to be from stock that had been kept pure for more than a hundred years. He was so staunch that he was worthless for hunting, as the first scent of game that he struck would invariably freeze him stiff, and nothing could stir him except brute force. I have frequently flushed and killed the bird to his point, and after gathering it, and showing it to him and vainly trying to induce him to move on—he all the while perfectly rigid—I have taken him by the collar and dragged him many rods away, only to have him, invariably, as soon as I let go of him, rush back to where he found the scent, resume his point to stay there, unless forced away, so long as the least vestige of taint was in the air. I have known him to remain for hours, as I several times left him to his fate, and would seldom see him until the next morning. I bred him to a very good-looking lemon and white bitch, very fast and a good fielder, but rather too delicate for rough work. The result was a fine litter of eight. I selected the subject of the sketch and christened him Trim. He was the best dog the world ever produced, and the best one that I ever saw. Hold on! I believe I have got that standard quotation a little mixed, but as it is gospel truth let it stand.

I had no end of trouble with him in his early days, as he did not take kindly to the course of instruction that I considered indispensable to his future well doing; it was literally a course of sprouts to him. After many trials, and much tribulation, I succeeded in teaching him to retrieve—when he had a mind to. I had no trouble in teaching him to charge, as that appeared to be his forte. He was the most listless pup that I ever saw, and could discount the original "lazy dog." I should have been utterly discouraged had I not seen him, when but nine weeks old, make several beautiful points on small birds; and on rare occasions I had seen him let himself out in wonderful bursts of speed. I was hungering and thirsting for a dog that would point his game in the same beautiful gamey style, and get around in the same lively manner, and so was very patient with him, hoping, almost against hope, that he would sometimes brace up and repay me for my trouble. I kept him until he was nearly a year old, when my mother, who had suffered long but not always in silence, emphatically told me that she would stand it no longer; Trim must go. Following close upon this dictum was a long list of his sins of omission and commission, the former consisting mainly in omitting to get up from his favorite place before the fire when any one was coming, and this performance had just ended, with herself as principal actress, in a wild whirl of dress goods and a sad mixing up of woman, dog and big arm chair. There was a light in her eye that I did not dare disregard; therefore, the next morning, early, I took Trim about three miles from home, to a farmer friend—who had vainly asked me for him several times, as he was overrun with woodchucks, and thought that the dog would rid him of the pests. I left him with him upon conditions that he should use him well, and return him to me in the fall when I commenced hunting. He thankfully received him and promised to take the best of care of him, and return him safe.

I must confess that my feelings on my homeward journey were far from agreeable. I had done a dishonorable act; I had foisted upon my unsuspecting and guileless farmer friend a worthless cur. How should I ever look him in the face again! On account of this feeling, I did not go to see Trim, and it was more than a month before I saw the farmer. It was with conscious blushes and a deep feeling of abjection that I responded to his cheery, "How fare you?" and was much surprised when he proceeded to laud Trim to the skies. "Why," said he, "I haven't fed him a mouthful since he has been there; he catches a woodchuck every day, and sometimes two, and don't eat anything else." I took an early opportunity to pay Trim a visit, as, notwithstanding his many faults, I had a warm place in my heart for him. I shall never forget the human expression of his eyes as he looked up to me when I spoke his name. My eyes were full of tears, and I put my arm around his neck, and did not speak for some time, and was just thinking that the farmer and his wife would think that I was foolish when he said: "Mary, I never saw such an expression in any eye, dumb or human, but once before in my life, and that was up under the big elm when I asked a certain little woman a certain little question, and she laid her head on my shoulder and looked just as that dog did; I really believe he's got a soul, and I don't wonder that the boy sets such store by him." This was many, many years ago, but the scene was impressed indelibly upon my memory, and oftentimes, with mental vision, I see that loving glance.

At the urgent request of the farmer I let Trim remain with him until the middle of November, when I brought him home and took him out for a hunt. If possible he was lazier than ever, and I had hard work to keep him with me; he would lie down and I could hardly start him. After a while he seemed to understand that it was either travel or trouble, and he followed at heel with a dogged look that did not augur very well for future usefulness. He paid not the slightest attention to the other dog, and when I killed a bird he took no notice of it whatever, and continued to act in this manner during several trips. One day when I saw him walk through a bevy of quails and the birds rose all around him, and he took no more notice of them than if they had been so many flies, I was utterly discouraged. On my way home I was thinking it over, and the more I thought the less I liked it, and I made up my mind that I would take him out the next day and shoot him. When I started out in the morning I told my father that I should leave Trim in the swamps unless he showed some signs. It was hard to make up my mind to this, but my patience was entirely exhausted, and I was heartbroken with his apathetic disposition. I hunted through the forenoon with fair success, and had eaten my lunch and was just ready to start when my other dog came to a point, right in the path; I walked in ahead and flushed a bevy of quails that flew straight down the cart-path, about thirty rods, and scattered in some low brush on the hillside. I followed and picked up several of them, when I happened to think that I had not seen Trim for some time; I whistled, but to no purpose, and started back expecting to find him, asleep, where I had eaten lunch, but when I got into the path, and looked up it, I was never more astonished in my life than to see this brute of a Trim on a staunch point, where the birds first started from. My mind was in a perfect whirl; I was completely dazed, and it was some little time before I stirred from my tracks. There was this dog, that had followed me around for two weeks with head and tail down, and had never in the whole time shown the least sign of intelligence, now wide awake, every hair bristling with excitement, his head well up, tail straight, and a magnificent sight as he stood in the open, just at the top of rising ground, his form outlined upon the clear sky, his jaws quivering with excitement, and every angle and curve of his body expressing eager desire. Here at last was the fruition of my long cherished wish for a dog that would make a stylish, gamey point. I walked up to him, and with many a loving pat and kind word endeavored to make him understand that I was in full sympathy with him, and that, thenceforth, I was his loving friend. It was laughable to see the other dog perform; although one of the best dogs to back that I ever owned, he was undoubtedly so much surprised to see Trim point, that he forgot all about it, and with a quizzical glance out of the corner of his eye up to me, he walked up to him wagging his tail, and for half a minute looked at him with such a comical expression that I could not help laughing; then he touched his nose to him as if to see if he were alive, and moved a step in front and suddenly froze in his tracks. I had supposed, until now, that Trim was pointing the old scent where the birds rose a half hour before, but knowing that the old dog would not do this, I began to think that there was more to the circus than appeared in the bills, so I stepped in, ahead, when up rose a quail that had been left. With a mental prayer that I might be loaded with straight powder I pulled the trigger and had the satisfaction of seeing the bird tumble. More than pleased with the whole performance, I loaded up and ordered the old dog to fetch, when Trim, with a rush like the swoop of an eagle, fairly distanced him, and picking up the bird returned, at a two-forty gait, and laid it in my hand without ruffling a feather. To say that I was happy does not express more than half of it; I was nearly delirious with joy, and I fear that I cut some foolish capers and said many silly things. It was nearly an hour before I felt steady enough to continue my hunt. Somehow I did not expect to ever see him make another point, and was very agreeably surprised, when I ordered the old dog on, to see Trim take the gait of a racehorse and quarter his ground like a veteran. He soon struck scent, and made a another beautiful point; the old dog backed him this time without any misgiving; I walked up to him and gave him a loving pat, when he moved on and I followed close to him for a quarter of a mile, and such beautiful roading I never saw before; he never showed the least doubt or hesitancy, but, with his head high in the air, followed the birds through brake and briar patch, and finally brought up at the edge of a small clump of bushes. After admiring his beautiful *pose* a moment I kicked the bushes, when up rose a full bevy of quails. I think that the excitement that I had gone through had unnerved me, as I did not harm a feather with either barrel. Taking a little time to recover my balance, I followed them up, and found them among some scattered birches. Trim behaved beautifully, of his own accord he took the wind, and with head up, he would unerringly locate every bird.

I had always considered the old dog as first rate, and he was a hard dog to beat, but he was just nowhere. Trim found all the birds and pointed them in grand style; his every movement was beautiful to see; talk of the poetry of motion; here it was exemplified. Every stride was a stanza, and every point that he made was a whole volume. It was with feelings of deep, heartfelt satisfaction that I wended my way home. I felt as though I was walking on air; I had visions of glorious sport in the future; henceforth I should feast my fill, and enjoy to the full that ecstatic feeling of almost perfect bliss that only he can know who has a perfect dog.

When I told my father in glowing language the result of Trim's last trial he did not entirely disbelieve me, as he knew that I always carried my little hatchet; but expressed a strong desire to go out with me the next day and see this paragon, and judge for himself. The next morning we were early afoot and soon arrived at the covert. Giving Trim the word he was off like a shot; we were in an alder run, some fifty yards in width, with a broad ditch running the whole length; Trim was covering the whole ground, leaping the ditch at every turn. We had proceeded some distance, when, just as he rose to clear the ditch, he struck scent, and, as he had not fairly extended himself for the leap, in he went neck and heels. When we got there we could only see the top of his head and the end of his nose; the rest of him had sunk in the mud with which the ditch was filled; but he had not broken his point; he was rigid as marble. After a little trouble I succeeded in getting across to where I could reach him, and, grasping his collar, I landed him on the bank and scraped the mud from him. He never moved a muscle, but, if anything, was more rigid than before. I stepped in to raise the bird, supposing that there must be one close by, when he carefully moved forward; we had gone but a few steps before I noticed that his style was altogether different from that of the day before; then he was magnificent; now he was glorious. Notwithstanding his bedraggled condition, he was a most beautiful sight and something wonderful to behold, as, with head high in air, his eyes protruding from his head, his mouth partly open and froth covering his lips, he followed the trail as I have often imagined the lordly lion moves on his prey; there was no noise and his every motion was perfect grace, and when, at last, he came to a stand and refused to advance another step we stood some time without speaking, drinking in with our eyes the wonderful picture. I broke the weird spell by advancing a few steps, when, with a mighty roar, up rose four or five ruffed grouse. Catching a glimpse of one that started to fly back, I whirled, and throwing my gun in his direction made a snap shot, and was rewarded by hearing that soul-satisfying thud as he struck the ground. Quickly loading, I bade Trim seek dead; he was off like a flash, and soon returned with the bird. I never saw a dumb brute express more pleasure than he; circling round me, with arched neck, he proudly carried the bird, and tried plainly to express his joy and to make me understand that this was his game. He was very loth to give up the bird, and after I had taken it he seemed so disappointed that I let him have it again, which pleased him very much, and he started off hunting with the bird in his mouth. We were very much amused to see him perform, and were greatly astonished to see him come to a point, still holding the bird in his mouth. Walking up to him he commenced roading, and followed the bird more than a hundred yards and finally brought him to bay in a corner. As I walked in ahead, the bird rose and I succeeded in bringing him down. After loading I attempted to get the bird still in his mouth, but he did not want to give it up, and to see what he would do I ordered him to seek dead; he soon found it, and dropping the one he had he picked up the one just killed and brought it to me, and, before I had a chance to say a word, was off and brought me the other one and gave it up readily. We concluded that he thought that the first bird was some rare specimen, and the only one that he would ever see, and he was therefore not going to lose sight of it, but finding that the "woods were full of them" he thought that I had better carry it. These were the first ruffed grouse that he had seen and I made up my mind that, although he loved them so well, he would prove their deadly foe—a prediction, I am happy to say, that was abundantly verified on many occasions in after years. They were emphatically his game, and although he was a remarkable quail and woodcock dog, and appeared to take great delight in their pursuit, their was not that earnestness, that high and lofty style that took possession of him as soon as he struck the scent of his favorites. A very enthusiastic friend, who shot with me a great deal, used to say that if I would bring him a single hair, plucked from Trim when he was on a point, that he could tell me what bird was before him.

There was an incident connected with this day's hunt that made a deep and lasting impression upon both of us; it was an exhibition of intelligence such as we had never witnessed before. Upon our return we passed through the alder run, and, on account of better walking, kept on the bank of the ditch, with Trim close at heel; when we arrived at the place where he fell in, he stepped in front and looking up at us, with a waggish expression in his eye and a positive grin on his face, appeared to enjoy the remembrance of his mishap of the morning; we both laughed heartily, and I am sure that the dog was laughing too. I am well aware that anything of this kind, when put on paper, loses a very large portion of its most interesting features; it is utter'y impossible to depict the eloquent expression of his eye, or the significant wag of his tail; the performances must have been seen to be fully appreciated.

Trim's reasoning faculties were of a high order, and I could give you hundreds of instances similar to the above, but for fear of being too prolix I will forbear; this being the first time that he had displayed this wonderful faculty, it struck us as being something remarkable. The day was a glorious revelation to me; I caught a glimpse of some of the possibilities of ruffed grouse hunting; hitherto I had hunted them, as almost every one does, in a haphazard manner, thanking the gods when I was lucky enough to bag one, and was not very particular how it was done, provided I got it. I liked the birds well enough but had always looked upon them as too wild and cunning for me, and had never spent much time upon them, devoting nearly all my time to woodcock and quails; but this day's sport had convinced me that there was a wealth of genuine, soul-satisfying sport in their pursuit that I had not dreamed of, and that no more royal game bird graced our forests, an opinion that has been strengthened year by year, and to-day I had rather take a good dog and follow up some old, wary cock grouse, even if I do not get him, than to bag a dozen woodcock or quails. Excuse this digression, as I am a little daft on the grouse question, and when I get a going do not know when to stop. There was one more revelation connected with this day that I caught a faint glimpse of that I must mention. I thought that I knew about all there was to be known about hunting, but before night I had the faintest suspicion of the fact that the dog knew more than I did about some things, and I had hunted but a few days with him before every doubt upon the subject was removed, and, ever after, when there was any conflict of opinion as to where the birds were, I let the dog have his own way. This was brought about by observing that when I was at fault in marking down a bird that Trim had ideas of his own upon the subject, which were generally correct; he was rarely at fault, and was possessed of a remarkable faculty for locating a flushed bird. He appeared to know intuitively just where it would alight. In vain would I try to make him hunt closer the particular bit of cover where I had seen the bird go down, and, after several times tramping the spot out myself to no purpose, he would, nearly always, lead me straight to the bird. Once, I shall never forget, I tried to make him go back and work over a corner that we had just come through, feeling sure that I had marked the bird correctly, and that it was lying close in there; he would not budge an inch, but looked back at me over his shoulder, slightly wagging his tail, and tried to induce me to follow to the next corner, a few rods to the right. I was vexed at, what I then thought, his sullen humor, and, breaking a stick, gave him a beating. As soon as I let go of his collar he made a bolt for the next corner, and came to a point just at its edge, and turned back his head to see if I was coming. I followed mechanically, feeling very uncomfortable, and that somehow I had done wrong. When I came up with him he broke his point, and making a detour tog et the wind, he soon had the bird fast. I stepped in ahead, and as soon as the bird rose I knew that it was the one that I thought I had marked so correctly, as I had shot at it and cut a feather or two from its wing, which caused it to make a peculiar whistling sound. At the first flutter of its wings, there was such a revulsion of feeling came over me as I wish never to experience again; dropping my gun l rushed back to the dog and throwing my arms around his neck tearfully promised him that never more would we have any misunderstanding. Trim appeared to realize what was passing in my mind; giving me a loving look, out of his wondrous, great brown eyes, he licked my face, some hing he had never done before. From this time forward we were in perfect accord, and I never allowed any doubt in my mind to influence me when he intimated to the contrary. As the season was far advanced I had but few more days' sport, but they were replete with a wonderful feeling of complete enjoyment, such as I had never experienced before.

Although Trim started off in such grand form he improved visibly every time we went out, and it was with deep regret that I hung up my gun at the close of the season. I was not aware how deep a hold my sporting proclivities had upon me, until I could no longer gratify them. So fascinating had been the sport, enjoyed in the last few weeks, it was a long time before I could think or talk about anything else.

Many moons waxed and waned, and still in my dreams the roar of the swift winged grouse, as they rose and burst through the tangled covert, only to be quickly brought down by my unerring aim, and the beautiful and unique position of Trim, as like Nemesis he silently followed them to their fate, gave me great consolation and made life, during the close season, not quite unendurable.

It was with happy feelings of glorious anticipation that my chosen friend and self, accompanied by Trim, sallied forth at early dawn on the first day of the open season. Would that I wielded the magic pen of a Herbert to describe to you the manifold beauties of that lovely morning, and to lead you, step by step, through wooded aisle and open glade, and to depict in glowing colors the many interesting scenes that were constantly transpiring; and, more than all else, would I wish to impart to yon a portion of the joyful feelings that to us were a continual feast; but as my pen is only a feeble one, at best, I will leave all this to your imagination. Suffice it to say that Trim more than verified the encomiums that I had lavishly bestowed upon him, and converted my friend from the error of his ways, woodcock-ward, and made him a staunch and lifelong devotee at the shrine of the lordly grouse.

There is no game bird in the world that so taxes the skill and patience of dog, and man, as a sly, old cock grouse; most fertile in cunning resources to evade you and escape, when, seemingly, you have him safe. In vain did they essay their most wily stratagems with Trim; he was up to all their maneuvers, and I could nearly always, tell what particular trick a bird was going to try on us by paying close attention to the dog. Did it attempt to run and gain the vantage of distance, from which to rise well out of shot, like a whirlwind Trim was after it, and passing on one side of it, a few feet ahead, he would turn and point as staunch as a rock, with the sadly demoralized bird between us. He would rarely fail in forcing the wildest of them to lie securely hid until, in numberless instances, I have literally kicked them from their hiding-place, so badly scared that the veriest tyro could easily have knocked them over as they floundered away in a straigit line, all the conceit, that they could twist and double, taken out of them. Did they endeavor to "swing round the circle" and get in our rear, and scare us almost to death with their infernal clatter, as they rose from the path where we had just passed, secure in the knowledge that if they heard the whistle of the shot it would not be in their direction, it was generally their last swing, for this performance had fooled us several times, and appeared to vex Trim, and so soon as a curve in the trail led him to suspect the trick, his hair would rise, and he would back out from the trail and swing for them in a manner that they did not appear to understand. Circling at break neck speed, until he got the wind of the now confused bird, he would hold it fast and give me an easy shot. His wonderful reasoning powers, and the tact which he displayed, in adapting himself to the different moods of the birds, were very prolific in filling the bag. Were they wild and prone to rise at a long distance, he would make as much noise as a pair of unbroken steers, and thrash around in the brush in a manner that strangers to him would always ridicule; but he knew what he was about, and approaching the bird in a serpentine course would get as close as he wished, and make his point, from which an avalanche could not stir him, and you could go home and get your dinner, with no fear but that you would find him there when you returned, and the bird too. Were they shy and disposed to skulk and hide, no cat more stealthy than he; with his head always high in air he would creep through the tangled thicket, never breaking a twig, nor turning a leaf, and if we did not get the bird it was not for the want of a fair shot. As an instance of his remarkable sagacity, I will relate an incident that was very pleasing to me, and that resulted in the capture of a most royal bird. It was just at the outlet of a large swamp, where there was a ditch about four feet wide, and as deep, that emptied into a small stream which it intersected at right angles; along the bank of the stream was an alder thicket that extended up stream ten or twelve rods and then curved round and joined the swamp; near the mouth of the ditch was a favorite spot from which I had several times started a noble bird, which had always got away scot free; it would manage to put the thicket between itself and myself, and fly close to the ground until out of shot. Bound to circumvent it, I took a friend and placing him on the bank of the creek, I took the inside, between the alders and ditch, and sent the dog in the thicket; he soon struck the trail, and followed it down to the ditch; I took my stand about a rod from the ditch and directed my companion to walk up to the dog and flush the bird, which he did, and the wiley old fellow, taking in the situation at a glance, dived for the ditch and flew so low that neither of us could see him. But he had played his last trick; there was a streak of dog and mud after him that forced him to show himself; a sullen roar, a cloud of feathers, and the gallant bird was beaten at his own game. Instead of standing perfectly still at the report of the gun, as he invariably did, Trim came directly to us, and, capering around us, plainly expressed his joy at the result; then going for the bird, he brought it to my friend first, and, arching his neck, marched around him in triumph two or three times, and then brought it to me. This was the first and last time I ever knew him to chase.

Trim was absolutely perfect in the field; there was no necessity to tell him where to go; he covered the whole ground, and, although a very fast and wide ranger, quartered his ground so close, and showed himself so often, that it was no trouble to keep track of him. At the faintest indication of scent he would come to a point and remain quiet until I came up to him, and when he had located his bird neither encouragement nor threats could move him an inch. At the rise of the bird, or report of the gun, he remained perfectly still in whatever position he happend to be, until ordered on. He was one of the best retrievers that I ever saw, both from land and water, never mouthing his birds, or ruffling a feather. I never knew him to bite a bird but once; we were hunting a wide belt of timber when my companion, at some distance to my right, signalled a point; I crossed over and, when nearly to him, flushed and shot a woodcock; at the report of the gun, a grouse rose before the dog and my friend dropped it close by the woodcock; both birds were only winged. Trim gathered the grouse first, when, coming in, he stumbled over the woodcock, which he saw was trying to get away, he dropped the grouse and seized the woodcock, then seeing the grouse making off he changed again; after swapping three or four times he deliberately shut his jaws on the woodcock, and, laying him down, picked up the grouse, and bringing him in returned and brought the woodcock and carried it straight to my friend, reasoning that he would not say a word, whereas, if he brought it to me, I might scold him for biting it. His conduct was the more singular, as he was very jealous that I should have all the birds, and no one could coax him to give up a single one. He was an indefatigable worker and disliked to stop a moment, but would work from morning until night; it was hard work to keep him quiet when I sat down to rest or eat a lunch. One day we had tramped a long distance, and coming out on the sunny side of the woods we sat down and took a long rest; when we got ready to start Trim was missing; I called and whistled, but he did not come; casting my eyes across the open lot I saw him two hundred yards away, at the far edge, pointing directly toward us. When we came up to him he broke his point, and wheeling round in the opposite direction led us a quarter of a mile away and came to a point at the edge of a stuble field; moving on we soon flushed a noble bevy of quail. It was plain to be seen that he had been there before, as his footprints were visible on the soft ground; he evidently reasoned that we would never find him, and, to let us know that he had found game, deliberately broke his point, and retracing his steps to where we could see him, pointedly told us to come along. This peculiar trait soon became habitual with him, and ever after we let him have his own way, knowing that if he found birds he would show himself and cause us no trouble to look him up. I found this habit very useful the next season, as, owing to a severe cut on my ankle, I was incapacitated from walking very far. I would sit in the wagon and let him go, whiling away the moments, like the "lone fisherman," in " glorious anticipation," keeping a sharp watch in every direction, and wondering at what point he would make his appearance. As game was very plenty I was generally rewarded by seeing him come bounding into open, and, after a stride or two, strike an attitude, the memory of which, even now, after the lapse of nearly forty years, causes my heart to bound with delight, and sends the hot blood tingling to my fingers ends. When Trim made a point there was a magnetic, inspiriting sympathy, amongst all beholders, that I can compare to nothing excepting to the sensation of an electric shock, and I have yet to see the dog that will cause my hair to rise to the elevation it obtained when viewing his performances. I cannot better describe this feeling than to quote the language of a wood-chopping Irishman, near whom Trim came to point. When we came up the man had dropped his axe and stood looking at him with heaving chest, gaping mouth and wide open eyes. "Look at him!" he said: "did yees iver see the likes of that; howly Moses, how my hair riz up and the cowld chills run up my back when he tuck the scent; if the howly virgin shud tell me there want twinty burds just forninst him, by my sow'l I'd belave the dog furst."

As an instance of his wonderful power of fascination I cannot forbear relating a little incident that afforded us many days of first-rate sport. We were hunting close to the farm of a man who never allowed shooters to set foot on his premises. Trim came to a point a few yards from the line, and as we came up to him we observed the man leaning on the fence, looking on. "Hold on," said he, "I want to come over and see that dog." We cordially invited him, and the old man became quite excited. "Why," said he, "I hain't been so woke up since my old stags runaway with the plow; see that consarned dog's hair turn toward his head—it beats all creation!" We flushed and killed the bird and the old man was perfectly delighted. After telling us he came out to keep us off his land, he gave us a pressing invitation, which he did not have to repeat, to go over and hunt in his woods, and he would go with us as he wanted to see that dog perform some more. It is needless to say that we went, and not only had a good time, but a good dinner, both of which were repeated on many subsequent occasions, for he urgently invited us to come again and to be sure and let him know so that he could go along and see the fun.

After a few seasons Trim gained a wonderful knowledge of the habits of the game he hunted, particularly his favorite, the grouse. After he had taken two or three turns in the cover he would almost unerringly, indicate by his manner, the presence or absence of game. Did he put on more steam, and hunt as though he expected to find game, you could take your oath that birds were near, or had been recently. On the other hand, did he slacken his pace, or express indifference, you might as well strike for some other locality as he was rarely mistaken. I soon discovered that he used his eyes as well as his nose, and, by closely watching him and profiting by his example, I soon became quite an adept in finding "signs." The faintest indication of birds, where they had scratched among the leaves, the plainly-to-be-seen wallow holes, where they had dusted themselves, a stray feather, their droppings, or the partly eaten skunk cabbage were to him as an open book that he literally read as he ran. Often have I seen him slow up and, glancing at the ground, throw his head in my direction and give me an expressive glance, accompanied by just the faintest wag of the end of his tail; then off again, at increased speed, he would seldom fail to soon find more tangible proofs of the presence of birds. Upon examining these places I would find unmistakable "signs," and soon learned to see them unaided by him. It is but a few days since I caused an incredulous smile to overspread the countenance of a friend, with whom I was out shooting, by pronouncing the cover we were in to be the home of a covey of grouse. We had gone scarcely fifty yards, and he was saying that he had hunted this cover for more than a dozen years and had never seen a grouse in it, when the dog came to a point and we flushed a splendid covey of ten or eleven birds, eight of which accompanied us home. It is a source of pleasure to me, as well as a cause of wonder to my sporting friends, that I am thus able to predict the near presence of game. This is one souvenir, left me by old Trim, that helps to keep him ever in grateful remembrance.

Nothing pleased Trim better than to get after a wiley old cock grouse. With what pertinacity he would stick to him! It was then that he put forth his greatest efforts, growing more eager at every rise, until, at last, when we had tired the bird out, or scared him so that we could approach near enough for a shot, his hair would turn toward his head and he would seem to expand to twice his usual size At such times he would turn his head until he caught my eye, when he would give me a glance of exultation that there was no mistaking. Ordinarily when I killed a bird, he would bring it in and lay it in my hand, with simply a wag of his tail; but when we got one of those wise old birds he would always arch his neck and proudly walk around me once or twice before delivering it, and had we extra hard work to circumvent one he would accompany his triumphant march with a joyful whine, or, as a friend expressed it, "Singing a pœan of victory." I shall never forget one famous chase after a magnificent old cock that led us a wild tramp upwards of four miles, straightaway, from the team, which we did not see again until after ten o'clock at night. We started him about two o'clock; he rose two hundred yards away, out from one end of an alder run as we entered at the other. I caught a glimpse of him as he swung over the tree tops, and got his course, which led into heavy timber, where we followed him a long distance only to see him pitch down from the top of a tall tree. Thinking that he would not "tree" again, I kept on; Trim soon found his trail, but before we got within fifty yards he was off again. He pursued the same tactics several times until my "blood was up," and Trim was more interested than I had ever seen him before; he raged around like a mad bull, the froth flying from his lips and his eyes glaring like those of a scared cat. It was now getting quite interesting, as it was nearly night; I still followed on, thinking that we must be getting the old fellow's wind, a supposition which proved correct, for Trim soon came to a point, and showed by his actions that he was close on to him. Stepping in front, great was my chagrin to hear this awful bird burst close to me, but on the other side of a bunch of laurel that I could neither see through nor over; I was mad, but nevertheless we went for him again. His next flight was short and we soon found him in a bunch of laurel. Making up my mind that something must be done, I made a rush for the bunch, and, as I went in, heard him derisely chuckle at me, and then, with victorious clapping of wing, he was off; but he little knew with what momentum I had charged that "forlorn hope." I got through somehow and was in time to "cut him down in his pride." How Trim's eyes did sparkle, and how his tail did wiggle! With what exultant feelings I proceeded to load, meanwhile, as was my wont, talking to Trim and telling him what mighty Nimrods we were. When Trim went to bring it I soon saw that it was only winged, but I had no fear, as it was impossible for a wounded bird to get away from him. As he was gone longer than usual I started after him and was much surprised to meet him coming back with head and tail clear down, and without the bird; when he saw me he sullenly led the way to a ledge of rock under which the confounded bird had taken refuge, secure as though he were a thousand miles away.

I will draw the curtain here; our woe was too sacred for profane eyes. It was now sundown, and to avoid the trackless forest I concluded to skirt the edge, as, although a mile or two further, it would be easier. We had gone but a short distance when from under an old tree top out went as many as twenty grouse; droping one right and left, I did not wait to load, but sent Trim after them. He brought them in, but so badly did he feel about losing that bird that the customary wag of his tail was entirely wanting, and he showed no disposition to follow up the birds just started, but gloomily followed close at heel. Not being very well acquainted with the ground, and as it was pitch dark, it took us four weary hours to get back to the team. Trim sulked all the way, and not even the memory of that beautiful double could dissipate the sadness from my mind.

The next morning, taking a friend along, we drove near to the place where I had started so many birds. As soon as we stopped to hitch the horse Trim bolted for the ledge at the top of his speed, and taking the trail of our wounded bird, which had left its hiding place, soon had it where tricks would not save its bacon, and bringing it to us, paraded around with it, whining with pleasure, and finally marched up to the horse and rearing up on his hind legs, held the bird for him to smell; then bringing it to me he barked and capered until our sides ached laughing at his comical performances. He had never barked before on any such occasion, but he felt so good that he had got the best of this, the wildest bird that we ever saw, that ordinary language failed to express his feelings, and several times through the day he would stop and look at us, a world of intelligence in his glance, and give two or three short barks, by which we, knowing that he was making remarks about his feat of the morning, would respond with words of praise which he appeared fully to understand. A year afterward, when in the vicinity of the ledge, he looked up in my face and used the same language, and I am confident from his manner that he retained a lively recollection of the affair.

I could fill volumes with interesting incidents connected with Trim's career, but I fear that already I have wearied the patience of the reader, and will say but a few words more. For many, very many long years I have been anxiously seeking the counterpart of old Trim; several times have I succeeded in finding something that came very near to him on some one kind of game, but I have never seen the dog that could compare with him for all kinds of birds; and for unflagging energy, combined with rare judgment, and, far more than all else, for speaking, almost human intelligence, he stands without a rival.

Graceful ferns, mingled with somber hued mosses, gently wave over his silent resting place; and, for more than a quarter of a century, as each golden Indian summer returns to us, loving hands have plucked from the graceful neck of the lordly grouse their beautiful plumes, and strewed his lowly bed with fitting tribute to the memory of him who loved them so well. SHADOW.

REARING PUPPIES.

WE receive many letters from different sections of the country complaining of want of success in raising puppies. Nearly all of them state that the writers have taken great pains with the animals and given them the best of care, but in spite of their efforts they sicken and die and, in many instances, entire litters are lost.

We have often thought that perhaps the great mortality complained of is owing in a great measure to this constant care and delicate nursing that anxious breeders bestow upon their pets. Who ever heard of a litter of mongrels that no one cared for meeting an untimely end? This we believe to be the key note of the whole matter, and that in order to be a successful breeder you must banish all fear for the lives and health of the youngsters, and let them shirk for themselves, and above all else give them no drugs or medicines of any description, for we are well satisfied that ten puppies are killed by dosing where one is benefited, and that the survivor is often ruined for long continued work by the injury thus wrought.

Now, we do not wish this to be construed as meaning that we are opposed to giving medicine at all times, for we are well aware that properly administered, much suffering is alleviated, and many valuable lives are saved, but we do firmly believe that the ailments of puppyhood should be left entirely alone, and that nature, if untrammelled, will effect ten times the cures that can be accomplished by the use of drugs, especially as administered by the breeders throughout the country who have no practical knowledge of their deadly effects, nor of the proper time nor remedy to apply in a very large majority of cases that come before them, but anxious to do everything in their power to save their darlings, and fearful that if something is not done at once the little thing will die, they, with the best intentions in the world, pour down his throat some powerful drug that but too often is sure to cause the very result they fear, and then, forsooth, they wonder why it is that the good die so young, and can only account for the success of their neighbor who raises every one of a mongrel litter by the fallacious reasoning that the blue bloods are of a higher organization, and consequently more delicate and harder to rear. That this is not true in most cases can be easily demonstrated by following the advice here given, and giving your high-toned litter the same chance for life that your neighbor gives his mongrels.

We are writing only concerning mature and healthy animals, believing that all who are otherwise should be religiously excluded from the breeding kennel. We have bred dogs for many years, and have been uniformly successful, at least so far as bringing our puppies safely through their early days is concerned, and we have accomplished this—or rather it has been accomplished—without any trouble or care upon our part by simply leaving them alone and trusting to nature the entire charge of their welfare. True, we always gave the mother plenty of healthful food and exercise, and as soon as the pups were a few days old removed them from their stall and made their bed upon the bare ground, and there they had to stay until they were weaned. We were often ashamed of their dirty appearance, but never of their health. We never wash a puppy. We do not believe that it is of any benefit to them, except in looks, and we believe it is often a source of trouble in that it induces a cold which may bring disease and death. Of course we keep them sheltered from cold and inclement weather, but at all times give them plenty of room on the ground, where they can dig in the dirt and get fresh earth to eat when they wish. After weaning, we accustom them to a diet of Indian or oatmeal, well cooked and mixed with plenty of thick sour milk. This we have found to be the best possible thing to expel the worms that many times infest them. It is also the best regulator of the bowels that we have ever tried, as by a little care in increas-

ing or diminishing the quantity it will always keep them just right. We frequently boil meat and use the broth for making their mush, and if their condition is not just to suit we give them an occassional meal of well cooked meat, and when their teeth begin to trouble them, we give them plenty of large bones, with a little meat on them, and never, under any circumstances—for their ordinary ailments—do we give them a single dose of medicine, and, above all else, we never worry our minds with thoughts or fears that they will not live.

We invite an expression of opinion upon this subject, and would like to see the question fully discussed in our columns, for, among the many trials and drawbacks encountered by breeders, none is more disheartening than to see the light fade from the eyes of their pets, as one by one they meet their untimely fate.

www.ingramcontent.com/pod-product-compliance
Lightning Source LLC
Chambersburg PA
CBHW021949160426
43195CB00011B/1290